Neurodiversity in Education

An Autistic Child's Journey through Mainstream School

By
Mabel Green

MAPLE
PUBLISHERS

Neurodiversity in Education

Author: Mabel Green

Copyright © Mabel Green (2025)

The right of Mabel Green to be identified as author of this work has been asserted by the author in accordance with section 77 and 78 of the Copyright, Designs and Patents Act 1988.

First Published in 2025

ISBN 978-1-83538-560-9 (Paperback)
978-1-83538-682-8 (Hardback)
978-1-83538-561-6 (E-Book)

Book cover design and layout by:
White Magic Studios
www.whitemagicstudios.co.uk

Published by:
Maple Publishers
Fairbourne Drive, Atterbury,
Milton Keynes,
MK10 9RG, UK
www.maplepublishers.com

A CIP catalogue record for this title is available from the British Library.

All rights reserved. No part of this book may be reproduced or translated by any form or by any means, electronic or mechanical, including photocopying, recording or by any information storage and retrieval system without written permission from the author.

The views expressed in this work are solely those of the author and do not reflect the opinions of Publishers, and the Publisher hereby disclaims any responsibility for them. This book should not be used as a substitute for the advice of a competent authority, admitted or authorized to advise on the subjects covered.

Children Learn What They Live

If a child lives with criticism, he learns to condemn

If a child lives with hostility, he learns to fight

If a child lives with ridicule, he learns to be shy

If a child lives with shame, he learns to feel guilty

If a child lives with tolerance, he learns to be patient

If a child lives with encouragement, he learns confidence

If a child lives with praise, he learns to appreciate

If a child lives with fairness, he learns justice

If a child lives with security, he learns to have faith

If a child lives with approval, he learns to like himself

If a child lives with acceptance and friendship

He learns to find love in the world.

By Dorothy Law Nolte

About the Author

Mabel Green is a mum to two children—one of whom is high-functioning autistic. Her family's often stressful journey through mainstream education has given her firsthand insight into how schools manage children who sit just on the edge of needing additional support.

Motivated by the lack of resources and understanding she observed over a decade ago, she trained as a teaching assistant. She began working with children with special needs in primary schools. Her goal has always been to support not just her child but others like them who may fall through the cracks in the system.

With a background in nursing, including 15 years of experience in hospitals and occupational health, she has a blend of medical, educational, and lived experience to her work. She also has insight into how the mental health system intersects with neurodiversity and parenting.

She believes passionately that there's a disconnect between what schools teach children and the real-world skills they need. Too many are pushed toward adulthood, feeling they're not good enough—something she's determined to change.

When she's not writing or advocating for neurodiversity, she enjoys gardening, creative projects, and relaxing with my cat.

Visit her at **www.neurodiversityathome.co.uk** or get in touch at **info@neurodiversity.co.uk**.

CONTENTS

1. The Introduction (First Encounter And Neurodiversity Definition)– 7
2. History Of Supporting Disability And Special Educational Needs– 17
3. The Impact Of The First And Second World Wars– 25
4. Then We Send Them To School– 33
5. Learning Difficulties In Mainstream School– 39
6. Measuring Ability - Mindset, What Is Intelligence and What Is Masking– 47
7. The Medical Model Versus The Social Model– 53
8. Who Is Responsible For Our Children - Safeguarding And Child Protection– 59
9. Equality, Inclusion And The Law (Lots Of Facts!)– 65
10. The SENCo– 79
11. Academies 85
12. You Are Going To Struggle With This. 93
13. Behaviour 103
14. What Did Inclusion Mean To My Son– 111
15. Childhood Trauma and Mental Health– 117
16. A Safe Place And A Parent's Journey– 125
17. Leaving Education - Employment And The Pipeline To Prison– 133
18. The Times Educational Commission– 139
19. The Education System In The UK– 143
20. The Future Of The Education System– 149

Mabel Green

Chapter 1

The Introduction

I started writing while I was a teaching assistant in a school but even before this time, I witnessed children falling through the attainment gap in the education system. They didn't fit the criteria laid down by the school that would qualify them for the support of a classroom assistant or one-to-one support in the classroom. Funding did not permit this. The sad thing is that there is a kaleidoscope of talent, skills and personalities who walk through our school doors and go largely unrecognised.

Many successful people say it's better to use our time and talent to work on our strengths rather than our weaknesses because that's what makes us unique, that's the reason we are here.

A child's inability to learn will rarely be due to their behaviour, motivation or compliance, which often seem like the same thing. The fact is that children may simply not be able to process the information presented to them. School work is assessed on 'ability', measured by what teachers observe and by how fast someone processes information. This, however, is not a measure of their intelligence. Being able to write at a certain age is not an indication of intelligence.

> Many clever dyslexics struggle to read
> There are clever ADHD children who struggle to sit and focus
> Some clever Autistic children take time to process information.

These things are not a measure of their intelligence. However, in the education system, children are assessed by work in exercise books and how they show up.

Our Children's Mental Health

We cram children with knowledge, putting them under increasing pressure to succeed, ignoring their individuality, emotions and unique mentality. The

Academies have invested so much in teaching that they have missed the point of what employers really want: emotionally balanced adults. Meanwhile, the Academies compete to see how many students they can have accepted each year, into the country's universities.

I have had issues with my son's education for most of his school life. I have witnessed the emotional cost of a misunderstood child who asked for help and who was left behind because no one listened or took the time to find out what his particular needs were, this quiet boy who loved learning and had plans to do a job that included his great love, science.

But this book is about more than my son; it could be about hundreds of children who have been failed by the education system. There are so many parents out there, trying to get support for their children. I am by no means the only one in this situation. Children who seem unable to cope or fit into the system will not fulfil their potential and end up with mental health issues because they have been denied control over their learning or lives.

My First Encounter

I worked as an Occupational Health Nurse at a computer company in my early thirties. The Department looked after the employees' wellness, offering first aid and delivering health and safety in their working environment. I noticed that some employee's folders had 'Dyslexic', 'Autistic' or had other specific learning differences identified. I had never seen this before as I had only worked as a hospital nurse. I asked why the files were marked in this way. I was told that the company valued this diversity in their workforce and encouraged different ways of thinking as it made for a more creative workforce. They were proactive in looking after their workforce as they recognised that the environment did not suit everyone equally and that people needed different types of support.

As time passed, I realised that many innovative tech companies worldwide did the same. Many wealthy business owners and entrepreneurs are Dyslexic, High Functioning Autistic or ADHD. While this is common knowledge now, in the nineties it was not.

The world's largest, most successful and innovative companies employ a neurodiverse workforce. This is not coincidental; it is strategic. If we want to create anything new, we need to embrace neurodiversity not as a challenge but as a valuable asset in the quest for innovation.

Autism, ADHD, dyslexia and other specific learning difficulties are only difficulties if our education systems label them that way.

Neurodiverse means that there are different ways that a human brain can work. We are all different, so we are all neurodiverse because we are all human.

As a nurse, I did my Cert Ed in Adult Education. I taught at Plymouth University for nursing students. Some techniques and methods enable a person to understand. I realised that this has two parts - Teaching, giving information and then receiving and processing that information. We all use our senses and our environment to learn. When someone gives me directional instructions, I write those instructions down. I find it easier to remember them if I can visualise. Hearing the words is not enough for me to remember or to carry out instructions later. I didn't fully understand this until my son started his learning journey.

We are born creative and curious, but yet we put our children through a standardised learning process. Where is the child in all this - SATs, league tables, GCSEs?

Adults decide what the children need to learn, not skills for the future. The future of this planet needs more than previous generations' thoughts and attitudes to survive. Teenagers campaign to save the earth, while many adults who can make a difference do nothing, or carry on with their destructive ways for short-term, gain. After all, it's not *their* future.

This book comprises my observations of my education experience and those of my children.

The Warnock Committee

In 1973, the Warnock Committee, led by Mary Warnock, was tasked by the Secretary of State for Education at the time, Margaret Thatcher, to review Special Educational Needs (SEN). Inspired by civil rights movements in America, parents of disabled children and those labelled as uneducable began advocating for their right to education. This lobbying culminated in the Education Act of 1970.

In 1978, the Warnock Report recommended the inclusion of children who required more support than their peers. These children might need additional physical, emotional, mental, or educational support. The report's recommendations became law in 1981, when policies and procedures were implemented to establish the SEN system.

After 40 years, have we truly understood what this means, and are we effectively implementing it?

Are we fostering a love of life-long learning, or are we creating adults who avoid re-training because of negative school experiences and suffer a lack of confidence, regardless of their potential?

We need to challenge these norms and think about what children need, rather than adhering to an adult-centric agenda. It's time to shift our focus from conformity to individual needs, and from standardisation to personal growth. This is not just a suggestion but a call to action for all of us to advocate for a more inclusive and effective education system.

Neurotypical vs Neurodiversity

Definitions:
- **Neurodiversity**: The natural diversity of the human brain.
- **Neurodiverse**: A group of people with different types of brains.
- **Neurodivergent**: A person whose brain functions differently from what is considered 'normal.'
- **Neurodiversity Paradigm**: The philosophy of neurodiversity.
- **Neurodiversity Movement**: The social justice movement.
- **Neurotypical**: A person whose brain functions are considered 'normal.'
- **'Normal'**: The standard, ordinary, usual, or what people expect.

Where did the concept of 'normal' come from?

The word 'normal' entered the English language around 1840. Before that, the closest equivalent was the word 'ideal,' which was considered the property of the gods—something unattainable for humans.

The use of 'normal' in the 19th century coincided with the rise of statistics. French statistician Adolphe Quetelet introduced the idea of averaging human features, such as height and weight, to define an 'average man.' Many statisticians sought to improve the human race, with some subscribing to the controversial beliefs of eugenics.

Origins of the Term Neurodiversity

The term 'neurodiversity' was first coined by Judy Singer, an autistic psychologist, to describe a movement advocating for the rights and recognition of individuals who are neurologically different. *(Source: Health Assured)

What does Neurodiverse mean?

- **Neurodiversity**: Diversity within the human brain.
- **Neuro**: Referring to the brain and nervous system.
- **Diversity**: Variety and difference.

Neurodiversity encompasses the natural variations in how human brains function. Our nervous system works with our senses—sight, hearing, smell, touch, and taste—to coordinate brain activity, influencing our thinking, learning, mood, motivation, and behaviour.

Being human means we all face challenges. These experiences help us learn and grow. As humans, we exist on a spectrum of intellectual and emotional abilities but not everyone fits societal norms.

The Need for Neurodiversity in Innovation

As we navigate an uncertain future, innovation and creativity are essential to address challenges like climate change and economic growth. The most innovative minds must collaborate to develop new ideas. Some of the most forward-thinking companies actively employ neurodiverse individuals, recognising the unique perspectives they bring. However, neurodiverse individuals cannot access these opportunities if schools fail to support their educational needs.

Challenging Standardisation in Education

We are all different. Every human has challenges they often try to conceal. Some children may not meet the criteria for specific learning difficulties but still struggle with dyslexia, autism, or other challenges, making reading or socialising difficult.

Standardised education often fails to accommodate this diversity, leading some children to mask their difficulties at great personal cost, including loss of education or social isolation.

Understanding learning requires acknowledging that no one is truly 'normal.' We are all neurodiverse. The current education system, with its rigid boundaries and restrictive curriculum, highlights deficits rather than celebrating differences.

The distinction between neurodiversity and Special Educational Needs arises from the medical model of society. Estimates suggest that at least 1 in 20 people are neurodistinct, with some research suggesting that up to 1 in 5 may be neurodivergent in some way. This includes conditions like autism, dyspraxia, dyslexia, and ADHD. (Source: *Uptimize*)

gaining-mainstream-traction

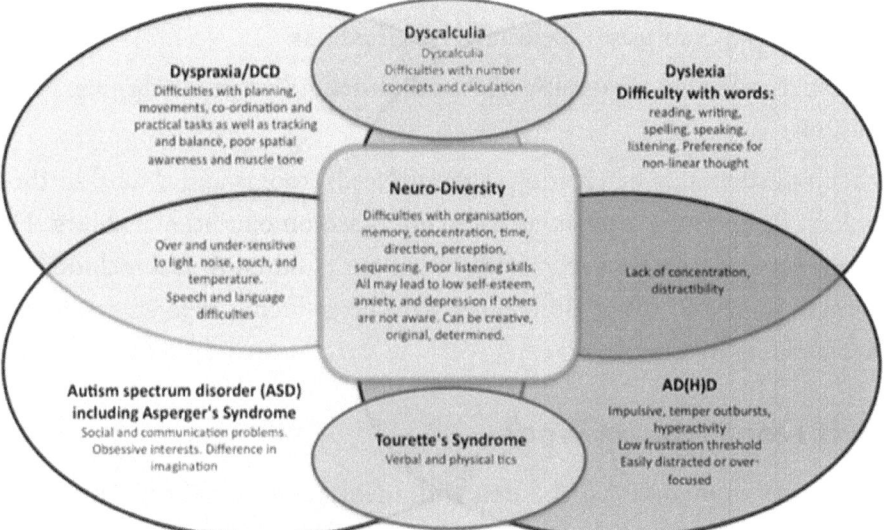

- ~8% of people in the UK are thought to have ADHD.
- ~10% of people in the UK are thought to have dyslexia.
- ~8% of people in the UK are thought to have dyspraxia.
- ~6% of people in the UK are thought to have dyscalculia.
- ~1% of people in the UK are thought to have an autistic spectrum condition.
- ~1% of people in the UK are thought to have Tourette's syndrome.
- It is thought that as research develops, certain mental health conditions such as psychopathy, some personality disorders, and schizophrenic conditions will come to be reinterpreted as having been diagnosed both in people who experience symptoms due to poor mental health and people who are experiencing neurodiversity and require different approaches to care.
- An additional ~3% of the population are known to have generalised intellectual disability.

- Some people believe that being generally intellectually gifted might be a form of neurodiversity, citing rare conditions like savant syndrome and hyperthymesia (highly superior autobiographical memory) as extreme examples of neurodiverse giftedness.

(Source: adhdaware.org.uk/what-is-adhd/neurodiversity-and-other-conditions)

Schools solve this by creating 'Special Needs' rooms and 'Hubs' so those who don't fit in have a separate place to go, based on educational ability. This doesn't seem like inclusion to me. We want our children to feel included and for others to respect their differences. Maybe reducing separateness would reduce bullying in schools.

Labels Don't Always Work

Carers of more disabled children with medical needs feel that labels don't accurately describe the challenges and fears they face. Autism is on a spectrum, so classification is required to accurately represent the different levels of need. This label covers a spectrum, from those who need constant care to those who can hold down a job. Treating a child or adult as an individual allows society to assess each person's needs without judgment. No two neurodiverse people are the same.

Parents often want labels so their children can get support in education they would otherwise not receive.

Neurodiverse or Special Educational Needs?

For some children with Special Educational Needs, the need is obvious, and support with an EHCP (Education, Health and Care Plan) and extra teaching support in a mainstream school is provided to aid their learning, such as those with profound autism or hearing impairments. Yet so many children are excluded because they are not supported as the individuals they are. The noise of a large year group could hinder the education of many children with good hearing but poor concentration. Restrictive teaching makes children who struggle with writing feel they are not clever enough because they are not producing the volumes other children achieve. Disruptive children are seen as time-wasters or naughty instead of anxious or having given up hope of keeping up.

Falling Through the Gap

Many children do not fit within the assessment criteria for support, but they are still struggling. They may be a bit dyslexic or a bit autistic and are left to cope. Educational support is only given to those with apparent problems or those seen as disruptive. The problem with this is that if help is given, it's sometimes too late for their education. There are not enough resources or knowledge, or in some cases there is an unwillingness to address the needs of struggling children as schools pursue their targets.

Carter Review for Initial Teacher Training (2016)

In 2016, the Carter Review for Initial Teacher Training added that Special Education Needs should be a core part of teacher training. The Warnock Report of 1978 planned to support Special Educational Needs in mainstream schools. My question is: can enough teachers identify the teaching and learning needs of the children in their classes?

Mabel Green

Chapter 2

A History Of Supporting Disability And Special Needs

Medieval Times (1050–1500)

Disability was as widespread in medieval Britain as it is today, yet communities demonstrated remarkable resilience in caring for people with disabilities. They understood the origins of disability as congenital conditions or acquired from diseases such as leprosy and years of hard physical labour. They used the words *Leper, Lame, Blynde, Deaff, Natural Fool,* and *Lunatick*.

Disabled children and adults were not left to fend for themselves but were cared for within the community, often within families or through marriage. Country folk supported each other in villages, fostering a strong sense of community and mutual support.

Churches and religious orders played a significant role in caring for those who could not contribute to the workforce. It was seen as God's work to care for the sick. Monasteries, nunneries and small hospitals provided care for those who were ill and infirm, demonstrating the impact of faith and compassion in history.

Between the 11th and 14th Century

Networks of small hospitals specialised in specific ailments such as blindness and deafness, as well as physical and mental disabilities. Those with these conditions lived and worked in communities supported by religious establishments. The attitudes of the day towards disability were mixed. Some viewed it as a punishment for sins, while others believed it was the consequence of being born under the influence of Saturn in astrology. Lepers enduring purgatory believed their sins were cleansed between Heaven and Earth rather than after death. Others saw disabled individuals as childlike and felt they were special for being closer to God.

The times of pilgrimages to holy places were believed to dispel curses or ease ailments, as noted in *The Canterbury Tales* by Thomas Becket. The less fortunate often ended up on the streets, begging alongside criminals and pickpockets.

The state did not provide support, so wealthy individuals seeking to feel virtuous or secure their place in heaven would donate money to support almshouses — *Maison Dieu*, meaning "Godly house," for long-term shelter for the disabled and aged infirm. This was seen as community service for royalty, noblemen, and wealthy merchants. The routine in alms-houses was strict, with rules governing lifestyle, diet and prayer, to save their inhabitants from a life on the streets.

From the 13th Century

At this time, the King had rights and duties of care over the "natural fools and idiots," those we know today as people with learning difficulties. He had custody over their property and assets and was responsible for their care. A special inquisition via county judges determined a person's mental state.

A declaration made during the reign of Edward I (1272–1307) defined certain feudal and political rights of the Crown, including the right to wardship of an idiot's lands to protect the idiot's heirs from disinheritance or alienation. This was also termed *de prerogative regis* (*dee pree-rog-[schwa]-tI-v [schwa] ree-jis*).

Leprosy communities were situated outside cities as society began to understand the spread of the disease. By the 14th Century, leprosy as a disease was receding and immunity was increasing, so these houses began to admit people with other disabilities.

The Black Death (1347–1350) created widespread fear about contagion and the spread of disease, leading to a more institutional response to disability

Mental Institutions

The first and most infamous mental institution was in London — the Priory of St Mary of Bethlehem, a charitable hospital in Bishopsgate, established in 1247. Initially run by monks caring for those with physical disabilities, it began admitting mentally ill patients, referred to as lunatics, in the 1370s. Today, we understand that people perceived as "idle" in such institutions often had learning difficulties.

For the next 400 years, most mentally ill people lived in village communities. However, scandals arose as more individuals outside religious orders became involved in their care. The City of London took over the management of St Mary's of Bethlehem due to poor administration, but the new governance led to charges of theft and embezzlement. Medical doctors, often with varying qualifications, experimented with treatments and medicines. Chains, manacles, stocks, and corporal punishment were used in misguided attempts to induce recovery or cure. The hospital later became known as Bedlam Hospital, giving rise to the term "bedlam."

Disability in Tudor Institutions (1485–1600)

Disabled individuals were cared for in religious establishments called "spittals" (hospitals) run by monks and nuns. However, concerns grew about neglect, abuse and the decay of buildings. One critic wrote, "I hear that the masters of the hospital be so fat that the pore be kept leane and bare enough."

In 1533, with Henry VIII's divorce and the split from the Catholic Church, many religious buildings and hospitals were destroyed. Treasures were seized, leaving many disabled people destitute and forced to live on the streets. Hospitals were plundered, and their staff killed. Henry VIII did not foresee the societal consequences of his actions.

London hospitals such as St Bartholomew's and St Giles Holborn were closed. Bury St Edmunds lost five hospitals, and a leper house and alms-house in Dover were converted into alehouses. When Henry VIII became aware of the increasing number of people on the streets, he restored some hospitals and alms-houses. Responsibility for care shifted from religious institutions to civil authorities and many establishments came under the control of city corporations, such as St Mary of Bethlehem that became the Royal Bethlehem Asylum.

The Poor Acts enforced harsh punishments on "lazy" criminals, but those born with disabilities — the blind, lame, or those "without wit or member" — were provided for by "overseers" with an allowance.

The 'Fool'

Henry VIII enjoyed the company of 'natural fools' at his court, using them to entertain him. As seen in portraits, he recognised them as part of his family. These individuals, whom we would now identify as having learning difficulties, served as an antidote to the betrayal and backstabbing in court life – and they were not truly fools; they were the eyes and ears of the King.

In 1547, the only institution left for the mentally ill after Henry VIII had finished destroying the religious institutions was Mary St. Bethlehem, now known as Bethlem Hospital. It was run by the Corporation of London, with medically trained superintendents. Mental illness required a cure, and treatment was a mixture of psychological, astrological, religious and traditional medicine.

Community Support

Most people with disabilities and learning difficulties still lived in the community. In Norwich in 1570, a 70-year-old blind baker ran a bakery with his wife's support. Thomas Bone, a 'dumb person', married Sara in 1618, marking the first English wedding conducted in sign language. In 1643, another deaf man, John Dyott, nicknamed 'Dumb Dyott', became a war hero. From the battlements, he fired a bullet that killed the commanding officer of the Parliamentary army; Lord Brooke returned home as a hero.

As a result of a 1570 census of the poor in the city, 63 of the 1400 poorest people in the city were identified as having disabilities — lameness, crooked limbs, blindness and deafness. They still worked as labourers and the women were skilled knitters and spinners. These individuals were part of the community; the parish paid a regular sum if their families struggled. When Alice Stock became too lame to work, the Parish of St Botolph of Bishopsgate in London paid her 6d a fortnight to look after her 'foolish girl' Martha.

The treatment of mental illness varied depending on one's financial means, and superstition still played a role in the causes and treatment of mental illness.

War

War brought casualties in the form of disabled men with horrific injuries, unable to work and left to die in the streets. During Elizabeth I's reign, the government began to provide pensions for soldiers and sailors. Those who had lost limbs were the first to benefit from an occupational pension scheme. Hospitals were built to house retired soldiers, and later, The Chelsea Hospital was established.

The Madhouses in the 18th Century

A notable feature of the 18th century was the rise of 'madhouses', private homes where people of lower social standing with dubious medical qualifications ran institutions. Mental illness was believed to be a 'loss of reason' that needed to be cured. Disability was viewed as misfortune, rather than being seen through the religious lens as a divine message or as possessing childlike characteristics.

Wealthy merchants paid for care in private houses, which boasted extensive gardens and indoor games for gentlemen and ladies, charging the highest fees. Meanwhile, people living in poverty were at the mercy of parish charity, often living in cold and filthy conditions. The *Gentleman's Magazine* of 1763 described 'cruel acts that went on in the madhouses', stating that many of these practices were 'arbitrary and unlawful'. A house in Winchester had private patients living in a mansion, while paupers lived in stables and outbuildings.

The 1774 Madhouse Act required all madhouses to obtain a license from a committee of the Royal College of Physicians and to be inspected annually. Some people locked away their spouse or relative in these institutions if they became a nuisance or if they wished to remarry. Private houses continued to make money by charging wealthy visitors to observe the 'lunatics'.

Under the Lunacy Act of 1846 and the County Asylum Act

In the same year, a commission was formed to regulate care, bringing asylums under the control of local public authorities. A resident physician was appointed and rules and regulations were enforced. The Home Secretary inspected each asylum, and care for mental illness and disability improved significantly.

Following the Great Fire of London in 1666, a large rebuilding programme was undertaken to display the new wealth of the city. New hospitals were built, and the Royal Bethlem Asylum was updated. A voluntary asylum movement grew, based on the idea that a clean, humane asylum regime would allow those with mental health issues and disabilities to flourish. Charles II wanted to replicate Louis XIV's *Hôtel des Invalides* military hospital in Paris, and so the Royal Chelsea Hospital was founded in 1682 for disabled and aged soldiers, and the Royal Hospital in Greenwich was established for disabled and senior navy veterans. In 1721, St Guy's Hospital was built in London for the incurably sick and chronic lunatics.

Schools

In the latter half of the 18th century, charity schools were established to educate children. Wealthy families had private tutors, but people with disabilities were unlikely to receive formal education. Schools for blind and deaf students began to emerge thanks to individuals fortunate enough to gain an education. Thomas Arrowsmith (1771–c1830), born deaf, attended a local village school. His mother had demanded a place for her son, and he excelled. Arrowsmith became the first child to attend England's first special school — Braidwood's Academy for the Deaf in Grove House, Hackney, London. He went on to become a well-known painter and artist, exhibiting at the Royal Academy. He set up two academies in Edinburgh and London and used his form of sign language, known as the Braidwoodian system, which became the forerunner of British Sign Language.

Edward Rushton's lasting legacy was establishing the Liverpool School for the Indigent Blind. After working on slave trading ships, he contracted contagious ophthalmia and lost his sight. Following an argument with his captain over the conditions of enslaved people, he was charged with mutiny. Upon his return, he became an anti-slavery campaigner and founded a school for blind students, which was second only to the one in Paris. The school taught music, spinning, and skills for the children to become independent after leaving.

Despite all this, most disabled adults and children continued to live in communities, working and being cared for by their families and the parish. The unfortunate ones were left to live on the streets, begging — known as 'Billies in bowls'

Victorian Asylums and Workhouses

The County Asylums continued with a resident physician, monitored by the Royal College of Physicians, with a few hundred patients. However, by the beginning of the 19th century, this was set to change. From just nine small charitable asylums, by 1900, there were 120 asylums in county pauper asylums, with an average intake of 1,000 patients, totalling 100,000, with an additional 10,000 in workhouses. Workhouses, also known as 'Public Assistance Institutions'.

In 1808, the County Asylum Act funded the building of County Asylums to remove the insane from the workhouses, but only 20 were constructed. Subsequently, 40 more workhouses were built to house those with mental health issues and those who didn't fit into society, including prisoners, not patients.

When we think of workhouses, we often recall the harsh conditions Dickens described in *Oliver Twist*. In 1834, with the 'Poor Law Amendment', workhouses became deliberately cruel and punitive. The authorities believed the 'idle' able-bodied were lazy and needed punishment. Many inhabitants were adults and children who would now be recognised as having disabilities or learning difficulties. Prior to this, workhouses had been humane communities, providing care for the disabled and destitute, and serving local parish needs, such as fire brigades, morgues, and meeting rooms.

The Poor Law Act of 1834

This Act led to the building of 350 workhouses across the country to punish the work-shy as the nation entered the Industrial Revolution. Some hospitals were opened, allowing patients to work on local farms and in kitchens. The patients repaired shoes and clothes to earn money. Many adults and children who never left these institutions did not have mental illnesses but simply had learning difficulties or were born to unmarried mothers

The Alienist

A new type of medical physician emerged during the Industrial period, known as the 'Alienists' — what we now call psychiatrists. They believed there was a cure for some mentally ill people, leading to cruel treatments such as electric shock therapy. However, the progress of new medicine slowed, and patients remained locked away, particularly the chronic and dangerous cases.

Self-help Groups

The rise of self-help groups for disabled people began during this period. The Guild of the 'Brave Poor Things', which had a coat of arms and a sword crossed with a crutch was one such group. Charitable schools for blind people and those who were deaf or hard of hearing also catered for other disabilities. Their motto was 'Happy with their lot', and they used military imagery to create positive feelings. They saw life outside as a 'battlefield', where pain was the enemy to be met and overcome through their daily challenges of securing food and shelter. By the end of the Victorian era, many charitable schools and organisations were providing services for disabled people. In 1868, Dr Armitage formed the British and Foreign Blind Association, which initially promoted the use of braille and later became the Royal National Institute for the Blind. Other charitable organisations offered education for 'lunatics', 'idiots', 'deformed individuals', and 'epileptics'. By 1899, 43 schools in London alone taught 2,000 children, meaning not everyone was destined for the workhouse.

Chapter 3

The Impact Of The First And Second World Wars

The First World War

The First World War had a significant impact on disability, as the injured men returning home demanded a new way of thinking. They had given their lives and bodies for their country and those that survived needed care. Inventions led to the development of prosthetic limbs and advances in surgery. With one million men killed and two million disabled, many required corrective surgery and equipment. Many ex-servicemen were unable to work and they received a pension. The 'King's Roll' was a 1919 scheme that encouraged firms to employ disabled ex-servicemen, but this initiative did not take off. Ex-servicemen worked in sheltered roles, such as making prosthetic limbs for other service personnel. In 1927, a driving trainer school where ex-service personnel became a taxi service in London.

Ex-servicemen received equipment and adapted housing for their disabilities, but unfortunately, this did not extend to the civilian disabled population. They were still living in colonies on the outskirts of towns and cities.

Eugenics

The 1913 Mental Deficiency Act set up a new board of control in line with the latest ideas of eugenics. Mental deficit colonies were scattered around the countryside, housing individuals who are now understood to have had learning difficulties and mental illnesses of various types. Children and partners were often separated and if possible, they were put to work within their communities in workshops, kitchens, gardens, and laundries. Education was compulsory for children, focusing on essential life skills, but they could never work outside the colonies.

Oxford Dictionary definition of Eugenics:
The study of how to arrange reproduction within a human population to increase the occurrence of heritable characteristics was regarded as desirable.

Primarily developed by Sir Francis Galton as a method of improving the human race, eugenics was increasingly discredited as unscientific and racially biased during the 20th century, especially after the adoption of its doctrines by the Nazis to justify their treatment of Jews, disabled people, and other minority groups.

Between and during the wars, the Germans also considered the mentally ill and those with learning difficulties to be a threat to the nation. There was widespread unease, as they feared these individuals might infiltrate the general population and weaken the nation's gene pool.

In 1930, Julian Huxley, a public intellectual, secretary of the London Zoological Society, and chairman of the Eugenics Society, wrote: "Every defective man, woman and child is a burden; every defective is an extra body for the nation to feed and clothe, but will produce little or nothing in return." Many political figures and prominent individuals, including Marie Stopes, who pioneered birth control, believed in this way of thinking. The 20th century was dominated by the notion of 'Human Perfectibility'. By definition, humans are not perfect.

After the Second World War

After the war ended, true horrors began to emerge. As a result of the persecution of Jews and the German torture of disabled people, the science of eugenics was heavily discredited. The pre-war ideas of isolating and sterilising disabled people, along with the Victorian notions of asylums lost favour, especially as scandals of neglect and abuse came to light. Over the years, newspapers and documentaries exposed the inferior treatment of those locked away and forgotten.

Rehabilitation, nursing, and advances in medical practices during the war led to the Disability Act of 1944, which promised shelter and reserved occupations for those returning from the war with disabilities. The National Health Service (NHS) was established in 1948, expanding the service to care for everyone, not just those who could afford it. The focus shifted to restoring fitness and mobility, teaching skills to help men return to employment and supporting mental health. Significant advances, such as artificial limbs and prosthetic fittings, became mainstream and spread to workers who suffered industrial accidents and helped those born with deformities.

Selwyn Goldsmith (1932–2011) became disabled with polio when he was 24 in the year he finished his architectural training. He fought against institutional discrimination and for adaptations for people with disabilities, including for those who were blind or deaf. After interviewing 284 people with disabilities in Norwich, Goldsmith built the first unisex cubic disabled toilets and fifteen ramped kerbs. While these designs seem dated now, they were groundbreaking for their time. He also authored *Design for the Disabled*.

"I wish, when I use buildings, to do so in the same way as others, to be integrated rather than segregated, to be treated as normal and not peculiar." — Selwyn Goldsmith, 1997

Sports

The birth of the Paralympics came about after a dressing competition at Stoke Mandeville Hospital. A Jewish Neurosurgeon and Nazism refugee, Ludwig Guttman, made significant breakthroughs with spinal injuries that had been thought hopeless. He gave them hope and a sense of purpose by getting them involved in competitive sports on the grounds. Guttman started with darts, skittles and snooker and expanded to wheelchair basketball and polo. On the day of the 1948 Olympics, Guttman organised his first competition against another local hospital. He also predicted that disabled people would have their own Olympics.

Phillip Craven became a world-class athlete following a climbing accident at 16. Motivated by his rehab he became an elite athlete. He took a British basketball team to the Paralympics in 1973. He removed the Paralympic image from medical rehabilitation and presented an elite class of athletes. Craven became the President of the Paralympic Committee in 2001. In the London Paralympics, 2,400 disabled athletes were participating in 20 sports.

Campaigning and Disabled People's Rights

Returning from war, ex-service personnel wanted to regain their societal roles and demanded a place. The National Cripples Journal blasted the government for its promise of security from the cradle to the grave but did nothing for the civilian disabled that could work and contribute to society.

In 1941 faced with an acute shortage in the workforce, the government recruited more than 300,000 unemployable (as they were labelled) disabled people under the heading 'Cripples Can do Vital War Work'. After both wars, they returned to their colonies outside the towns and cities.

Many new campaigning organisations and charities formed. The National Association for Mental Health and the National Association of Parents with Backward Children started in 1946, becoming MIND and Mencap. Other charities established themselves, such as Leonard Cheshire Foundation, British Epilepsy Association, and the Spastics Society, now known as Scope. Marches through London in 1951 started a social movement and many charities started campaigning for disability and civil rights.

In 1961, Enoch Powel declared that all the Mental Health Hospitals, as well as Asylums and Workhouses, were to close over 15 years in favour of developing Hostels in the community instead. The Ministry of Health wrote a report: A Hospital Report for England and Wales and the Development of Hostels but it would take 25 years to see this happen.

Camphill Communities

In 1940, a group of Austrian refugees settled in Scotland to set up a community for children with learning difficulties. A paediatrician, Dr Karl Koenig, was inspired by Ralph Steiner's Principles of Living. With the financial support of wealthy local families, they set up a community that supported children and adults with learning difficulties so they could get an education and a purpose in their lives.

Mental Health issues and Learning difficulties

The 1944 Disability Persons' Employment Act promised employment for those returning from the war, teaching daily living skills. Slowly, it filtered down to the existing disabled population, helped by the formation of the

National Health Service in 1948, but this was a slow process. The advances in rehabilitation supported those with industrial injuries.

The Education Act of 1944 and the formation of the Local Education Authority (LEA)

The aim was to remove inequalities in the education system by offering poorer children a place at Grammar schools. This only sometimes worked, as families could not afford the extra cost. Also, the Local Education Authority(LEA) formed and was answerable to the new Department of Education.

They provided three types of schools - Grammar, Secondary Modern and Technical schools. The choice allowed every child to fulfil their potential following an 11-plus exam. The leaving age was 15 years, then in 1972 this was raised to 16 years old after 'O' level exams. Within this act, they still saw children with learning difficulties of all levels as not being fit for education, labelling them 'Ineducable'. In 1955, the Guild of Teachers of Backward Children was established to teach children labelled as 'Subnormal and severely subnormal. In the 1959 Act, the term 'Backwards' was frequently used,

In 1959, the Mental Health Act replaced the Mental Deficiency Act.

People should only be voluntarily admitted or, if they were a danger to themselves or others, they would 'be sectioned'. The NHS soon realised that half the beds were being used for mental health illnesses or issues. The level of spending was going to be a factor in how effective the move from institutions into the community would be.

The Beginning of the End

These asylums and hospitals had always been places prone to scandal and abuse; they were not lovely places. Sadly, information is still coming out about historical abuse. The first hospital to close was Banstead Hospital, and then most of the Asylums closed as medical treatment and as public opinion changed. Many people were discharged with no experience of outside life and with no skills to cope with the outside world. Some admissions were for medical reasons, such as epileptics or women who had a baby out of marriage.

60's and 70's the civil rights activists

People with disabilities gathered strength and campaigned against discrimination of poor access and for equality. The Union of the Physically Impaired against segregation (UPIAS) and the Mental Patients Union(MPU) started campaigning against being in residential care and asylums instead of their families.

https://disability-studies.leeds.ac.uk/wp-content/uploads/sites/40/library/UPIAS-UPIAS.pdf

Between 1960 and 1980

During this time, Asylums were closing and government passed Acts to move towards more community-based care.

National Assistance Act 1948

Health Visitors and Social Work (Training) Act 1962

Children and Young Persons Act 1963

National Health Reorganization Act 1973

Children's Act 1975

National Health Service (Vocational Training) Act 1976

Local Authority Social Services Act 1970

Mental Health (Amended) Act 1982

to list a few

Following the Seebohm Commission in 1968, the Local Authority Social Services Act 1970 created the framework we know today. The government created departments in local areas to assume the responsibility for local Authority Health and Welfare Services. These services co-ordinated social care, involved the families in their homes and reached out to the community for support. Patients were to live with their family or have assisted living, learning life skills and vocational courses in the community.

Autism and Learning Difficulties

This book focuses on the journey made by people with Autism and Learning difficulties. Learning disabilities and mental disorders seem often to be intertwined. When the Asylums closed, the health and social welfare system had many different needs to cater for. Those seen as different were no longer lumped into one place and shut away. Each person's care and welfare was planned according to their needs. People were starting to think about how they fitted in. Were they simply not able to, or was society not accommodating them?

The Disability Discrimination Act (1995)

The Tory government of John Major passed the first piece of legislation that protected those with disabilities and people with learning difficulties against discrimination. Many existing acts were superseded, such as - the Race Relations Act 1976 and the Gender - Sex Discrimination Act 1975. However, there was no protection for those with a disability that was life restricting like people with Learning Difficulties. This act covered Education, Health Care, and Employment.

Mental health after the closure of the asylums

Society has largely neglected mental health and learning disabilities/difficulties. Their needs and rights are sometimes similar. Due to underfunding and lack of priority, in my opinion, the mental health support in this country has a long way to go to match its physical counterpart in the NHS.

The latest monthly Assuring Transformation NHS Digital data shows that in April 2023:

- In total, 2,060 autistic people and people with learning disabilities were in inpatient mental health hospitals in England.
- 1,320 (64%) of these people were autistic
- 225 under 18s in inpatient units were autistic or had a learning disability. Of these, 96% were autistic.

Despite some progress in moving people with learning disabilities out of hospital and into the community, the number of autistic people in inpatient facilities had increased. In 2015, autistic people made up 38% of the number in hospitals; in 2023 it was 64%.

https://www.acamh.org/blog/autism-resources-update/

http://mulberrybagsau2012.com/number-of-autistic-people-in-mental-health- hos-3.html

Chapter 4

Then We Send Them To School

We are all individuals with our own agendas and perceptions of the world. We use our senses to observe and evaluate what's going on, along with our intellect and social and cultural values. We are creative beings and happiest when we are doing what we want to do and being the people we want to be.

I love how children start to see themselves by drawing their arms and legs out of their heads, with big hands and feet. They draw the body parts that they use and that are essential to them. As time passes, children realise they are people in their own right, with their bodies, feelings, thoughts, and opinions. Eventually, they feel they have the power to achieve whatever they want.

We allow our children to fantasise about what they would like to be when they grow up and we try to facilitate their dreams and wishes. Every child has the right to an education.

Before the invention of schools

Thousands of years ago, we 'played' and 'explored' our environment and learnt how to live as hunters and gatherers. There was no distinction between playing and working, with groups or families working as a team, teaching survival skills. Children were supported in roles they enjoyed or were good at within the family. Children taught themselves to learn through exploration.

Society changed when we lived in buildings and created villages, towns, and cities. Agriculture, industry, and religion-imposed boundaries and structures, forcing children to become products of what society wanted them to be. Agriculture saw children as a workforce, expecting long hours of toil to feed a family and extra to barter with. Factory owners gave children repetitive and low-skilled work instead of time to play. The pressures of society forced families to work harder, as children were the ones that earned them more money. Any spirited, rebellious child not conforming to the rules of work would be punished or end up dead.

At the turn of the century, during the Industrial Revolution, families often comprised of many children who had to work. The poorer you were, the more children you had available to send to work; if one died, you had another. In 1833, the Factory Act protected children under 9 years old from being part of the workforce. Hours were limited to a maximum of 48 hours a week for those under 12 years old, and under 17-year-olds were restricted to 69 hours working in conditions harsher than we can imagine.

In those times, a child's individuality and creativity were not important. They needed to be obedient and to do the will of their master. In 1898, education in England became compulsory as there was a need to train children for a future workforce. Tedious repetition and testing were seen as character-building, preparing children for this sort of work in the future.

Religious schools filled children with fear that if they didn't follow the scriptures or adhere to what the schoolmaster thought was acceptable behaviour, they would be punished.

Not every child adapted to factory work or labour in the fields, but they had to follow the rules. If they strayed, there was a punishment. They had no choice but to work. In those times, adults assumed that to get a child to learn, some had to be punished to be shown the right way. Even now, children are only allowed out to play to let off steam, and as they get older, play is not part of the learning process, except in activities like 'Forest School' and Physical Education.

The Victorians saw teaching the three 'Rs' and working in the local factory as all the child needed to do, not valuing individuality. The illiterate were left behind to fend for themselves.

In the early postwar years, the formation of the Local Education Authorities (LEA) offered three types of schools: Grammar, Secondary, Modern, and Technical. The different types of schools were for 11-year-olds, with the 11-plus exam determining grammar school entrance. It led to most primary schools adopting streaming from an early age. Robert Smith, who taught in a Sheffield primary school just after the war, recalls, "The scholarship class was streamed according to ability in arithmetic and English. We worked them hard, and about 10% were selected for grammar school."

However, in 1967, the Plowden Report finally pushed primary schools into the modern age, introducing ideas from psychology, child development, social equality, and welfare. Children were no longer seen as empty vessels but as individuals who responded to different learning styles.

Robert Smith, then a young primary headteacher in Oxfordshire, is the only surviving member of the Plowden committee. Today, he recalls its willingness "to ask very fundamental questions." Unlike today's government-commissioned inquiries, Plowden gathered evidence widely, including from abroad, and achieved political consensus.

The sentence catches its essence: "At the heart of education lies the child". According to Smith, "That was fundamental, the idea that education should be related to individual differences, especially the range of intellectual ability and children's capacity to learn at different rates". This relates to children's varying ability to process information through their preferred senses.

The late 1960s and 1970s were the high point of "progressive" education; schools were not bound by a national curriculum or Sats (standardised assessment tests) in Year 2 and Year 6.

But by the 1980s, there was a political backlash, partly provoked by extreme examples such as the William Tyndale primary school in Islington, London, which became notorious for allowing children to do as they liked during lessons, including watching TV or playing table tennis. Was it poor management or poor interpretation of Plowden's inspired policies?

Plowden Report

In relation to the curriculum, the Plowden Report was clear: 'One of the main educational tasks of the primary school is to build on and strengthen children's intrinsic interest in learning and lead them to learn for themselves rather than from fear of disapproval or desire for praise.' The report's recurring themes are individual learning, flexibility in the curriculum, the centrality of play in children's learning, the use of the environment, learning by discovery, and the importance of evaluating children's progress – teachers should 'not assume that only what is measurable is valuable.' (Derek Gillard - infed.org/mobi/the-plowden-report)

The Curriculum

This backlash ended with the creation of the national curriculum under Margaret Thatcher's government and has led many, ever since, to see primary education as a battle between opposites: child-centred or subject-centred, progressive or traditional, informal or formal, a broad curriculum or the "three Rs".

School and Education are not the same thing.

School is all about learning and remembering facts, obeying rules, and passing tests. Education comes from the Greek word 'educo', which means "to draw out", facilitating an individual's talents, abilities, ideas, and gifts. To develop from within.

Compare and Grade

We teach children by reinforcing their differences, grading them, and comparing them to each other. We constantly reassure children that failure is not bad because there has been a history of measuring children as we squeeze them into a system. In the process, some children will lose their individuality, creativity and sense of who they are. We now have children who feel the pressure of needing to achieve. Is it any wonder that there is a massive increase in mental health issues?

This system of 'One size fits all', emotional intelligence and bullying are only given lip service and inclusion doesn't work.

"My contention is that creativity now is as important in education as literacy, and we should be treated with the same status." "We are educating people out of their creative capabilities." (Sir Ken Robinson - TED Talk - *Do schools kill creativity?*)

How many adults fear furthering their knowledge and skills because they failed school because some teacher told them they could have been better at something or because they were tested against other children with different talents and did not cope with the comparison? We are creating a population of future adults who need to learn what they *can* do because they are measured and tested in areas they are not interested in and are not allowed to explore their talents.

I see a standardised curriculum being planned by Trusts and given to all primary schools within a 'Multi Academy Trust' without any consideration of the differences in children. A teacher knows their pupils and can plan accordingly. Many know that 'One size fits all' education turns children into winners and losers. Children pass or fail by a measure designed by civil servants that defines education regardless of a child's talent and what they can contribute to society.

The Education and the 'Medical Model' defines the boundaries regardless of a child's differences to make the system work. They will then struggle and feel the fault or defect is with them.

Going into an unknown future where technology changes exponentially, we need creative minds who can think outside the box. The next generation needs to be trusted to develop new solutions to problems we have yet to learn about. Teachers are teaching children who will be going into a future that they, as teachers, have no idea about and will not be part of. Children of today understand the emerging technology of the future. Are we restricting the future's talent and creativity by using outdated educational priorities?

We may need to turn the education system on its head and put the child's needs first.

Plowden is a voice from the past but one which urgently need to be heard again today. When politicians realise that what is measurable is not all that is valuable, when teachers begin to notice that children learn nothing by being tested, when parents are sick of their young children suffering from exam-induced stress, when the public begins to realise that the results of national tests can always be manipulated to achieve politicians' targets and when decent people decide to stand up against the name-and-shame culture of failure, then someone, somewhere, is going to remember that 'at the heart of the educational process lies the child.' The Plowden Report still stands as an valuable analysis of the needs and possibilities of the primary school. (Derek Gillard - infed.org/mobi/the-plowden-report)

Who's Responsible Now?

The Academies plan the curriculum and manage the schools in 'Multi-Academy Trusts'. While OFSTED regulates and assesses the schools, who are the Academies really answerable to?

Chapter 5

Learning Difficulties In Mainstream School

Learning difficulties, learning disabilities, and intellectual disabilities seem to be interchangeable depending on the country research originates from. A difficulty usually becomes a disability when it starts to have an adverse effect on a person's health and social well-being.

A disability is described in law (the Equality Act 2010) as 'a physical or mental impairment which has a long-term and substantial adverse effect on a person's ability to carry out normal day-to-day activities.' Formally known as 'Mentally Handicapped,' learning difficulties are categorised in four ways:
- Mild learning difficulties
- Moderate learning difficulties
- Severe or profound learning difficulties
- Specific learning difficulties

Mild Learning Difficulties

Children with mild learning difficulties manage in school, where they can converse and communicate their needs. Early identification and appropriate support for their speech or specific learning difficulties can empower them to achieve their potential.

Moderate Learning Difficulties

Some children may have speech difficulties and achieve at a level significantly lower than their peers. They may also find it challenging to acquire literacy and maths skills, have low concentration levels, and underdeveloped social skills. The support given can provide employment and a fulfilling life.

Severe or Profound Learning Difficulties

Children with severe or profound learning difficulties, including those with Profound and Multiple Disabilities (PMLD), have complex needs. However, they are not alone. With an EHCP (Educational Health and Care Plan) and the involvement of various agencies, they can receive the support they need, providing reassurance to their parents and educators.

Learning Disabilities

The 2001 White Paper on the health and social care of people with learning disabilities, known as *Valuing People*, included a comprehensive definition of learning disabilities. This document was a significant milestone in the understanding and support of individuals with learning disabilities, shaping policies and practices in the UK.

Valuing People defines learning disability as:

'Learning disability includes the presence of:

- a significantly reduced ability to understand new or complex information, to learn new skills (impaired intelligence), with;
- a reduced ability to cope independently (impaired social functioning); which started before adulthood, with a lasting effect on development.'

Mainstream Schools

Moderate, severe, and profound learning disabilities are usually apparent to those in education and health, and support is hopefully organised so a child can have an education either in a special school or mainstream school. An EHCP can meet the child's needs within the Educational, Health, and Social Care system. Labels are essential for parents to define the issues their child is experiencing.

With an educational system that is so structured – one size fits all – you can see why this is happening. Teachers don't always have the experience to spot issues or know if it's a learning difficulty, leaving the parents wondering if their child has a problem. Getting a label means that the school needs to support a child under the Special Educational Needs Code of Practice 2014. Children are individuals, and we are all on the neurodivergent spectrum, so it makes sense that only a portion of the school population can tune into the learning.

Those who are gifted and talented are not pushed to reach their potential; those who are just a bit dyslexic, a bit autistic, or a bit different just lose out.

Mild Learning Difficulties

I am talking about mild learning difficulties that become invisible in mainstream schools. The critical point here is that this does not affect their intelligence.

Specific Learning Difficulties

In education, this refers to children who have specific learning difficulties such as dyslexia, dyscalculia, and dyspraxia.

Dyslexia

You usually see a child who is doing well in all but one of their subjects. The specific difficulty could be reading and writing, but the child is so knowledgeable about so much that it doesn't measure up.

Dyscalculia

A child may be good at English, reading, and other subjects but needs help grasping maths.

Dyspraxia

Once labelled 'The Clumsy Child', a dyspraxic child may struggle with coordination, such as catching a ball, walking in a straight line, or sometimes leaning against a wall as they walk down a corridor. These children can be slow to pick up a pen due to poor gross and fine motor skills and sensory processing issues. Underneath all that, given time and support, they are competent children who can achieve a good education.

Autism

Autism is a neurological disorder that's on a spectrum. Some high-functioning children are clever, while others may have mild to profound disabilities. They present with restricted or repetitive behaviour, struggle with social communication and interaction and may experience sensory overload from their environment. Many autistic children may also have specific learning difficulties such as dyslexia, dyspraxia, or ADHD.

There are around 700,000 autistic people in the UK, and they are as individual as everyone else.

The Diagnostic Criteria

In 2013, the American Psychiatric Association updated its criteria for autism in the DSM-5 (Diagnostic and Statistical Manual of Mental Disorders). They also included a social communication disorder, Social (Pragmatic) Communication Disorder (SPCD). Many children just miss the autistic criteria as they exhibit only some of the characteristics and may show many of the repetitive and restrictive behaviours. The problem is that many children learn to mask their behaviour to fit in and so miss being given the diagnosis they need.

The categorisation of autism no longer uses different labels; instead, there are three levels of needs:

- **Level 1** (formerly Asperger's) requires support, and these children are likely to be in mainstream school.
- **Level 2** requires substantial support.
- **Level 3** requires very substantial support.

Level 1 (formerly Asperger's) – "Requiring support"

- **Social communication:** Without support in place, deficits in social communication cause noticeable impairments. These include difficulty initiating social interactions and clear examples of atypical or unsuccessful responses to the social overtures of others. The person may have decreased interest in social interactions.
- **Restricted, repetitive behaviour:** The inflexibility of behaviour causes significant interference with functioning in one or more contexts.

Switching between activities is difficult. Problems of organisation and planning hamper independence.

Level 2 – "Requiring substantial support"

- **Social communication:** Marked deficits in verbal and nonverbal social communication skills; social impairments are apparent even with supports in place; limited initiation of social interactions; and reduced or abnormal responses to social overtures from others.
- **Restricted, repetitive behaviour:** The inflexibility of behaviour, difficulty coping with change, or other restricted/repetitive behaviours appear frequently enough to be evident to the casual observer and interfere with functioning in various contexts.

Level 3 – "Requiring very substantial support"

- **Social communication:** Severe deficits in verbal and nonverbal social communication skills cause severe impairments in functioning, with very limited initiation of social interactions and minimal response to social overtures from others
- **Restricted, repetitive behaviour:** The inflexibility of behaviour, extreme difficulty coping with change, or other restricted/repetitive behaviours markedly interfere with functioning in all spheres. Great distress/difficulty changing focus or action.

The American Psychiatric Association 5th Ed Diagnostic and Statistical Manual of Mental Health Disorder

ADHD – Attention Deficit Hyperactivity Disorder

ADHD affects a person's behaviour, making them impulsive, hyperactive and lacking concentration. This disorder could be a specific learning disorder related to how people learn, but it doesn't affect a person's intelligence. Sometimes, in school, it takes work to measure.

What is the difference between ADD and ADHD?

There is no difference between ADD and ADHD. ADD (attention-deficit disorder) is an outdated term for what is now called ADHD (attention-deficit hyperactivity disorder). Some children with ADHD exhibit hyperactive behaviours, while others do not, but the diagnosis is ADHD either way.

Source: ChildMind.org - What is the difference between ADD and ADHD

Executive Functioning

Executive function and self-regulation skills are the mental processes that enable us to plan, focus attention, remember instructions, and successfully juggle multiple tasks. Just as an air traffic control system at a busy airport safely manages the arrivals and departures of many aircraft on multiple runways, the brain needs this skill set to filter distractions, prioritise tasks, set and achieve goals, and control impulses. We don't have to have a learning difficulty to struggle with one of our executive functions or self-regulatory skills. You only need to see a child after they've had lunch with too much sugar!

People with learning disabilities tend to struggle with executive functions, as we all do to a greater or lesser degree. Issues vary for people who have specific learning difficulties such as dyslexia, dyspraxia, autism, and ADHD, as well as those with syndromes such as Down's syndrome, for example. Our brains are unique, but we all have blank spots and could benefit from support with our executive functioning.

Executive Functioning Skills

- **Planning**: The ability to figure out how to accomplish our goals.
- **Time Management**: Having an accurate understanding of how long tasks will take and using time wisely and effectively to accomplish a task.
- **Working Memory**: The mental process that allows us to hold information in our minds while we work with it.
- **Self-control**: Regulating yourself, your thoughts, actions, and emotions.

- **Perseverance**: The ability to stick to a task and not give up even when it becomes challenging.
- **Organisation**: The ability to develop skills to manage a system that keeps plans and materials in order.
- **Task Initiation**: The ability to independently start a task even when you don't want to.
- **Metacognition**: Knowing what you know and applying that information to learn.
- **Attention**: The ability to focus on something or someone for some time and shift your attention when needed.
- **Flexibility**: The ability to adapt to situations as they change and deal with the change.

Source: Understood.org - What is Executive Function

Processing Information

When we learn, we receive information through our senses: our eyes, ears, smell, taste and touch. We use these organs to receive information, but the brain interprets it and gives us the answers or results of our findings. Many people with learning difficulties have varying processing difficulties, which often go unnoticed.

A child sitting in a classroom may struggle with how the teacher presents information. We all have our ways of learning through our senses or learning styles. I know my child is 90% visual and 10% auditory. A noisy classroom can make it difficult for him to take in what is being taught and he may appear not to understand. Many children know how they learn; it's such an innate skill, but their individualities are not valued. They just have to sit and listen.

Teachers use 'multi-sensory' methods, but that doesn't cater to those who aren't quick enough to keep up with their weakest senses or get overstimulated visually. The whiteboard is the main focus of learning. You don't have to have a learning difficulty or a statement to struggle with this 'one size fits all education'.

Children with processing disorders can learn if given the teacher's time and support, such as lesson notes. Children who have issues with executive functioning skills can learn techniques to manage themselves in the classroom and on the playground.

Sensory Processing Disorder (SPD)

In specific learning disorders, autism, and ADHD, children get stressed and anxious because they can't regulate their senses in the world they live in. They cannot block out or calm their response to noise or visual stimuli. All their senses are on high alert, so they struggle to cope, get overwhelmed, or don't respond. Equally, their senses may be under-stimulated, so they don't respond. My son is not deaf but doesn't process quiet noises efficiently; with touch, some children need to be hugged or can't cope with wearing clothes. Many children have a mismatch of hypersensitivity and hyposensitivity.

A child may seem slow or not understand a piece of information. Their reaction to a stimulus is out of proportion, and this is called Sensory Processing Disorder (SPD).

Three Patterns of Sensory Processing Disorder

1. **Sensory Modulation Disorder**: The person has difficulty responding to sensory stimuli – they may be overresponsive, their senses overwhelmed, or under responsive, not registering a reaction or craving the stimuli.
2. **Sensory-based Motor Disorder**: The person may have poor balance, coordination, and motor skills, and struggle to be aware of where their body is in relation to the world around them.
3. **Sensory Discrimination Disorder (SDD)**: This person may need help understanding stimuli, how to use them, or figuring out which way to turn when walking.

An excellent book on the subject is *The Out-of-Sync Child: Recognising and Coping with Sensory Processing Disorder* by Carol Stock Kranowitz.

Chapter 6

Measuring Ability

Dr Carol Dweck, a professor of psychology at Stanford University, wrote a book, *Mindset: The New Psychology of Success*, in 2006. She introduces the concepts of fixed and growth mindsets, describing how children with a fixed mindset believe they cannot change the outcome of their learning experience. How does this impact their mental health?

Mindsets

There are many mindsets, as there are different types of intelligence, but the main ones we deal with in school are the 'fixed mindset' and the 'growth mindset'.

Issues with a Fixed Mindset

- Decreased self-knowledge
- Reduced risk-taking
- It causes unhealthy competition, being hypersensitive to lack and scarcity

Growth Mindset

- Intelligence, abilities, and talents are achievable.
- They choose to challenge themselves.
- They can stick to a challenge and persevere.

Infants of preschool age who are happy and secure in their worlds would have a growth mindset, believing they can achieve what they want. They decide they want to learn to walk and they don't give up if they fall over; they stand up and try again. People around them listen to their dreams and they are encouraged. A child sees another child riding a bike and wants to learn. Children know what they are interested in and with some, you can see potential musicians or sportspeople. Those children don't understand the concept of failure; they just try again if this is a skill they want to master.

When children start school, they learn to fit in and conform to a system that has very fixed expectations of them: control, conform, and cram. The ideas of failure and comparison are shown to them as they are tested and compared to their classmates. Actions speak louder than words, so the fixed mindset of the education system is what the children hear, while the teachers verbally reinforce the positives of having a growth mindset. We learn more from the examples presented than from what we verbally hear.

Learning from Failure

We need to fall in love with failure. Children come to school not fully understanding failure, but it is explicitly explained as they are judged and compared to their classmates. Much of our mental health issues stem from our poor attitude towards failure. Children in distress do not have the tools to cope, but we can help them learn from their mistakes. We could turn their failures into successes, but to do that, the school agenda needs to be more flexible. Learning from failure is a powerful tool that can empower and motivate educators and parents in their roles.

Much of our compulsory education comes from the need for societal control and a workforce. We need to give our children the tools to think for themselves. The old ways of educating the masses are incongruent with this time in our evolution.

Our parenting attitudes have evolved, so why hasn't the education system changed? This stagnation should not be accepted. It's a challenge that educators and policymakers need to address urgently and overcome, to improve our children's education. The need for a shift in the education system is crucial and cannot be ignored.

Keeping the education system running as it always has is not keeping up with present-day and future workforce needs. Children need knowledge, but they also need skills to survive. Knowledge is at their fingertips via their phones and mental health issues are on the increase.

What is Intelligence?

Intelligence can be defined in many ways: higher-level abilities (such as abstract reasoning, mental representation, problem-solving, and decision-making), the ability to learn, emotional knowledge, creativity, and adaptation to effectively meet the demands of the environment.

Psychologist Robert Sternberg defined intelligence as "the mental abilities necessary for adaptation to, as well as shaping and selection of, any environmental context" (1997, p. 1) https://www.simplypsychology.org/intelligence.html

The TED Talk by Sir Ken Robinson discusses how teaching affects a child. The education system is designed to support academia, with a protracted university entrance process. I laughed when I first heard Sir Ken Robinson talk about how the education system teaches our children, but it's not funny. He describes how we get our children to sit down, teach them from the waist up, only use their heads and prioritise the right-hand side of their brains. What happens if a child wants to use the rest of their body?

This system measures the intelligence required to get a job based on 19th century needs. Sir Ken Robinson also describes how very talented, creative students think they are not intelligent because they need to excel in the subjects that the education system has defined as intelligent—maths, sciences, technology, and engineering. The 'creative' subjects are only sometimes valued or, at worst, stigmatised.

IQ (Intelligence Quotient)

The intelligence quotient is the measure of mental ability and intelligence. Tests and assessments that measure cognitive, reasoning, and logical thinking skills. The average score is around 100, and those who score high can be members of Mensa—an organisation admitting those with 140 and above, about 2% of the population.

EI (Emotional Intelligence)

Emotional intelligence is all about understanding our ability to manage our emotions, to perceive, use, and understand them. Being in control of our feelings can help us with our interpersonal relationships, enhancing our personal and professional lives.

Daniel Goleman defined emotional intelligence in 5 ways:

1. **Emotional self-awareness** – knowing how one feels
2. **Self-regulation** – controlling and directing one's emotions
3. **Motivation** – achieving goals through enjoying the learning process and perseverance when meeting obstacles
4. **Empathy** – sensing others' emotions
5. **Social skills** – managing positive relationships

Daniel Goleman – *Emotional Intelligence: Why It Can Matter More Than IQ*

We need to rethink what intelligence means.

Howard Gardner's Multiple Intelligences

In 1983, Howard Gardner, an American developmental psychologist, described nine types of intelligence https://www.howardgardner.com/multiple-intelligences:

- **Naturalist** (nature smart)
- **Musical** (sound smart)
- **Logical-mathematical** (number/reasoning smart)
- **Existential** (life smart)
- **Interpersonal** (people smart)
- **Bodily-kinaesthetic** (body smart)
- **Linguistic** (word smart)
- **Intrapersonal** (self-smart)
- **Spatial** (picture smart)

Masking, What is it?

Masking refers to the behaviour of individuals with autism who consciously or unconsciously copy social behaviours to be socially included. A person might mimic facial expressions, gestures, tone of voice or other social cues that may not come naturally to autistic individuals as learned behaviour. This is a coping mechanism that allows individuals with autism to navigate social situations more smoothly. It reduces social anxiety and avoids negative judgement or rejection.

Girls can be more socially aware, so they learn to copy appropriate social behaviour. Many more boys are diagnosed with autism compared to girls, as girls seem to blend in and cope, but at what cost? Masking can help individuals with autism manage social interactions but can become mentally and emotionally taxing. The effort to constantly monitor and imitate social behaviours may lead to fatigue and stress. Many children hiding their autistic characteristics don't get the support they need.

I knew my child was hiding behaviour that enabled him to decompress when he was feeling sensory overload, but the school did not believe me. He worked hard to manage himself in class so the other children wouldn't laugh at him, but he wasn't coping inside.

Mental Health Concerns

People who have to hide their actual behaviour and constantly monitor their actions will feel on edge. There are significant effects on a person's mental health, both short-term and long-term.

Increased Stress and Anxiety

Masking requires constant effort and vigilance to monitor and imitate social behaviours that may not come naturally. This effort can lead to heightened stress and anxiety, as individuals worry about making mistakes or being "found out."

Mental Fatigue

The cognitive load of constantly monitoring and adjusting behaviour can be mentally exhausting. Individuals who 'mask' their behaviour experience fatigue, affecting their overall well-being, as they cannot relax and be themselves.

Feeling Isolated

Masking may lead to isolation, as individuals may feel they are not truly understood. Maintaining a facade can create a barrier to forming genuine connections with others, leading to a lonely life.

Impact on Self-Esteem

Constantly masking one's authentic self can contribute to diminished self-esteem. Individuals may feel they need to hide certain aspects of their identity to be accepted.

Burnout

Over time, the effort to mask can contribute to burnout. Individuals find it challenging to sustain the level of social mimicry required, leading to exhaustion and a potential decline in mental health. Increasing anxiety takes its toll on other things in their life, such as schoolwork and progress in their job.

Delayed Diagnosis and Support

Masking can sometimes make it more difficult for others, including professionals, to recognise the signs of autism. The result can be delayed diagnosis and a lack of appropriate support and accommodations.

Masking creates a mismatch between inner feelings and outward appearance

Masking can create a significant disconnect between an individual's internal experience and how they present themselves externally. It's essential to recognise the impact of masking on mental health and well-being. We need to create environments that foster acceptance and understanding.

Chapter 7

The Medical Model Verses The Social Model

The world expects things to work; if something is broken, we want it fixed. The medical profession works towards fixing broken or different people who need to fit in. We have a set of values and attitudes defining what is 'normal' and aspire to be that. Social media sets out the rules of what we should wear, act or do, if we follow them. These guidelines define society and can dictate the usual.

So why be normal?

What's wrong with not being normal? We are all covering up our insecurities, which can lead to many mental health issues.

Accept differences because we are all different.

Disability has become a health issue, a discrimination issue and a human rights issue.

Ways of Viewing Disability

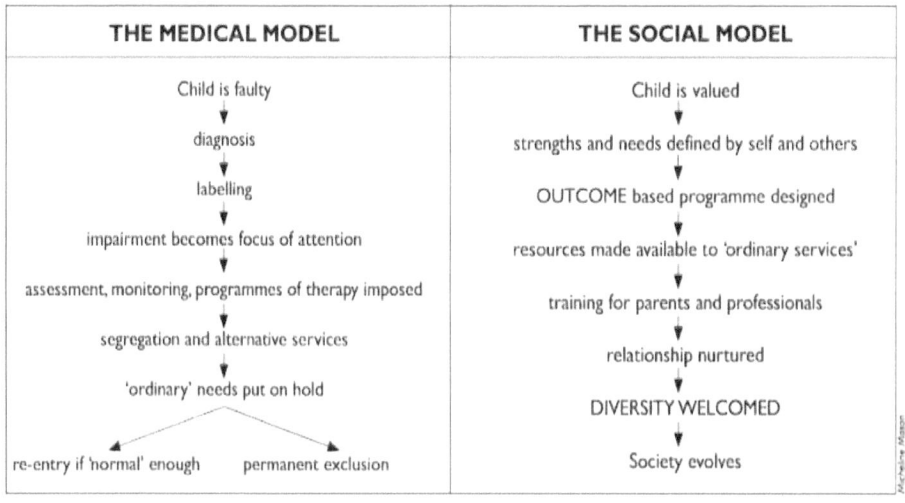

The Medical Model

The medical model is led and defined by medical opinion. People are labelled by their illness or disability, and they need to be fixed. Their reason for living becomes about having treatment to change themselves to fit in with most of society. The abnormalities and dysfunctions make up their diagnosis, and doctors and scientists see this as unfavourable. Labels and diagnoses set people apart as different via a defined assessment and criteria, with segregation and alternative services provided.

Disabled people are seen as damaged, broken, and in need of fixing or curing. They don't fit the standard mould and need to be changed or, as history has explained, shut away and excluded from society.

Definition of Disability under the Equality Act 2010

You're disabled under the Equality Act 2010 if you have a physical or mental impairment that has a 'substantial' and 'longer term' negative effect on your ability to do normal daily activities.

- 'Substantial' means more than minor or trivial, e.g., it takes longer than usual to complete a daily task like getting dressed.
- 'Long term' means 12 months or more, e.g., a breathing condition that is a result of a lung infection.

https://www.gov.uk/guidance/equality-act-2010-guidance

Some disabled people need caregivers to support them in their daily lives as they are unable to function in the 'normal' world. They have to fit into what is defined as standard in society because they are different.

Other disabled people don't need a caregiver to support them in their daily lives, but they have a minor disability that affects their function in society, such as a learning difficulty.

The Medical Model

The medical model defines people as being held back by their impairments, and society's expectations measure their deficiencies. They look at what is wrong with the person and what sets them apart from the average person. The person is judged through their impairments and not the human being underneath. It's all about fitting in to survive.

The medical model looks at what is 'wrong' with the person, not what the person needs. We believe it creates low expectations and leads to people losing independence, choice, and control in their lives. – scope.org.uk

The Social Model

Sociologist Michael Oliver was the first Professor of Disability Studies in the UK who wrote and taught about disability for social workers. As a disability activist, he further promoted the ideas of the Social Model of Disability.

Vic Finkelstein, born in South Africa, was a wheelchair user from the age of 16. Imprisoned for his apartheid activities, he later came to Britain as a refugee. Vic was a tutor at the Open University, continuing his activism with disability. He was one of the founders of Disability Arts and the Disability Rights Movement. He was one of the leading writers of a document that put forward the idea of disability being created by social barriers, starting with the concept of the 'Social Model'.

The social model of disability is a way of viewing the world, developed by disabled people. The model says that people are disabled by barriers in society, not by their particular impairment or difference. Barriers can be physical, like buildings not having accessible toilets, or they can be caused by people's attitudes to difference, like assuming disabled people can't do certain things. – scope.org.uk

Social Model

The Social Model believes that society creates barriers that dis-enable people. These barriers are attitudinal, environmental, organisational, and communicational.

A 'reasonable adjustment' is a change to remove or reduce the effect of:
- an employee's disability so they can do their job,
- a job applicant's disability when applying for a job.

(www.equalityhumanrights.com/en/multipage-guide/employment-workplace-adjustments)

Attitudinal Barriers

What society defines as 'normal' creates judgment and values that people use to understand their world. Society can be as exclusive or inclusive as it wants to be. Fads and fashions can make people feel at ease or uncomfortable with their peers if social media defines them. If society defines specific values as usual or 'normal', then everything outside those values is not valued or accepted. People start to feel abnormal or excluded.

Organisational Barriers

Disabled people can go to work and live a 'normal life' if they can access places of work and leisure with dropped kerbs and lifts. Policies and procedures allow people to be safe in their workplace, regarding employment, managing their work hours and using assisted technology with a clear understanding of their role.

Physical Ability Barriers

When people are prevented from leaving their homes they become dependent on others if their environment is unsafe. Someone partially sighted or deaf people may be unable to navigate their way to work, alone. A dyslexic person may be unable to read signs or write their name. An autistic person may feel anxious about meeting people as they struggle to understand and navigate their way within social groups and their work environment may be sensorily overwhelming.

Communication Barriers

Communication barriers create issues but that doesn't mean they cannot do a job. Understanding or processing information quickly enough, as seen with people who are high-functioning autistic, doesn't make them less intelligent.

All these forms of communication can affect how someone communicates, but assisted technology and a little time and understanding can make life easier.

Valuing Diversity

We are all different and have individual needs that need valuing. The survival of any species depends on diversity and adaptation. People who think differently have a lot to offer this ever-evolving society. Many technological companies, such as Google, value people who are neurodiverse because they believe that creativity solves problems that an atypical employee may not see. Many minds work together to design future technology.

The Social Model accepts differences.

Every person needs to be valued. We have equal rights and access to society with free choice, autonomy, and informed consent to live our lives.

The Social Model believes a person is not disabled; they are dis-enabled by the barriers in their life. The community or employer can adjust to support, because everyone has design faults that need support. That makes us human.

Support is made available to those who need it without discrimination and judgment. Labels and diagnoses trap them: "I am me, and you are… autistic!" A label brings with it so many judgments, opinions, and discriminatory beliefs.

"Factors in a person's environment that, through their absence or presence, limit functioning and create disability. These include aspects such as:

- a physical environment that is not accessible,
- lack of relevant assistive technology (assistive, adaptive, and rehabilitative devices),
- negative attitudes of people towards disability,
- services, systems, and policies that are either non-existent or that hinder the involvement of all people with a health condition in all areas of life."

https://www.cdc.gov/ncbddd/disabilityandhealth/disability-barriers.html

Support and Education

Sometimes, a label is useful as it brings difficulties to the attention of others, helping them to get support. Many people struggle or fail because those around them do not understand the challenges they face.

The catch is that those who are 'atypical' or fit the 'normal' standard need to be more considerate and understanding, especially if they are in positions of power, in schools, hospitals and the police. Some hospitals still use the term 'mental retardation' to identify someone with learning difficulties. More education is needed to recognise behaviour and provide appropriate support.

If you have no insight or knowledge, you have no clue.

Legislation that Recognised Disability

- The Chronically Sick and Disabled Persons Act 1970
- Disability Discrimination Act 1996
- Equality Act 2010
- United Nations Convention on the Rights of Persons with Disability 2008

https://www.open.edu/openlearncreate/mod/oucontent/view.php?id=148890&section=2.4

Chapter 8

Who Is Responsible For Our Children Safeguarding And Child Protection

What is Parental Responsibility?

All mothers and most fathers have legal rights and responsibilities as a parent, known as 'parental responsibility'.

If you have parental responsibility, your most important roles are to:
- Provide a home for the child
- Protect and maintain the child

You're also responsible for:
- Disciplining the child
- Choosing and providing for the child's education
- Agreeing to the child's medical treatment
- Naming the child and agreeing to any change of name
- Looking after the child's property

Parents must ensure that their child is supported financially, whether they have parental responsibility or not.

(gov.uk - Parental Rights and Responsibilities)

- **Who is Responsible for Education in the UK?**

The Department for Education

The Department for Education (DfE) is responsible for children's services and education, including early years, schools, higher and further education policy, apprenticeships, and wider skills in England. The DfE is a ministerial department supported by 18 agencies and public bodies.

(gov.uk - Department for Education)

The Right to Education

It wasn't until 1970 that disabled children – previously classed as being unable to be educated – were given the right to participate in education, through the Education (Handicapped Children) Act 1970. (Legislation.gov.uk - Education (Handicapped Children) Act 1970). However, the law has changed substantially since then: Protocol 1, Article 2 of the Human Rights Act, Article 28 of the UN Convention on the Rights of the Child, and Article 24 of the UN Convention on the Rights of Persons with Disabilities all state the right of disabled people to receive an education.

Young people, with or without a learning disability, must now be in education or training until at least the age of 16. In England, they must then do one of the following until they are 18:

(gov.uk - Know When You Can Leave School)

- Stay in full-time education, e.g. at a college
- Start an apprenticeship or traineeship
- Work or volunteer (for 20 hours or more a week) while in part-time education or training.

(Mencap - Your Child's Rights in Education)

Academies' Responsibilities

Academies in England are responsible to the Department for Education (DfE) and its agencies, as well as for charity and company law. The DfE devolves authority to Academy trusts through its legislation and funding agreements, and the trusts are held accountable through the contract with the government. Academies are also subject to educational and financial oversight from the DfE's National and Regional Schools Commissioners (RSCs), their teams, and the Education and Skills Funding Agency (ESFA).

Academies are not-for-profit private trusts owned and run by boards of trustees. The trusts are responsible for the staff, assets, and land of the schools they run, and the staff become employees of the trust. The trusts also have a CEO and executive leadership team overseeing multiple academies and supporting individual academy leaders.

Academies are subject to the same inspection regime, test and examination performance measures, and primary legislation as other schools. Ofsted inspects and rates their performance transparently on Ofsted's website and the DfE's performance tables.

Defining Duty of Care

Schools have a duty of care to all pupils, including:
- Pupils who are on the school's roll part-time (dual registered)
- Pupils with special educational needs (SEN) or disabilities
- Pupils with medical needs

While there are no absolute duties under legislation or common law, school staff must take all reasonable steps to ensure children are not exposed to unacceptable risks. A teacher's duty of care was historically often described as the teacher acting 'in loco parentis'.

The Meaning of 'In Loco Parentis'

A Latin phrase which means 'In the place of a parent'. The legal responsibility of a person or an organisation, such as a school or nursery, that takes on the role and responsibilities of a parent. They must take reasonable care of themselves and the children in their care.

Safeguarding and Child Protection

What is Safeguarding?

Safeguarding is the action taken to promote children's welfare and protect them from harm.

Safeguarding means:
- Protecting children from abuse and maltreatment
- Preventing harm to children's health or development
- Ensuring children grow up with the provision of safe and effective care

- Taking action to enable all children and young people to have the best outcomes

What is Child Protection?

Child protection is part of the safeguarding process. It focuses on protecting children identified as suffering or likely to suffer significant harm. This includes child protection procedures, which detail how to respond to concerns about a child.

(learning.nspcc.org.uk - Safeguarding & Child Protection)

Child Legislation

The protection of children legislated in law started in 1880, protecting the interests of children around the time of the Industrial Revolution and child employment, just before the beginning of compulsory education. There has been a long history of implementing legislation and guidelines since 1945 in response to cases of child abuse and murders at the hands of their abusers. Content reviews continue to update the system covering children and vulnerable adults.

The Children Act of 1948

Under this act, Local Authorities had a duty to provide care to help children when parents could not or if it was in the child's best interest.

In 1973, reforms were needed.

There was a public inquiry into the death of 7-year-old Maria Colwell when she returned home from foster care. Her stepfather killed her, and the system failed to protect her. The result was an improvement in the system, highlighting the need for a greater understanding of and identification of signs of child abuse, leading to the Children Act of 1975.

Timeline of the History of Child Protection

https://learning.nspcc.org.uk/child-protection-system/history-of-child-protection-in-the-uk

Significant changes to safeguarding policies and guidelines continued after the death of 8-year-old Victoria Climbié, which led to Lord Laming's report (2003). This report led to sweeping changes in the way children's services were organised in England and Wales. It changed how education, social care, and health work together.

The publication from the Government, *Keeping Children Safe in Education*, was first published in 2015 and is updated every year.

gov.uk - Keeping Children Safe in Education

www.gov.uk/government/publications/keeping-children-safe-in-education--2

Safeguarding Children and Child Protection

All organisations that work with or come into contact with children should have safeguarding policies and procedures to ensure that every child, regardless of their age, disability, gender reassignment, race, religion or belief, sex, or sexual orientation, has a right to equal protection from harm.

Setting up and following good safeguarding policies and procedures ensures children are safe from adults and other children who might pose a risk. This includes voluntary and community organisations, faith groups, private sector providers, as well as schools, hospitals, and sports clubs.

Mabel Green

Chapter 9

Equality, Inclusion And The Law (Lots Of Facts!)

What Does Inclusion Mean?

Noun

1. The act or state of including or of being included within a group or structure.
2. The practice or policy of providing equal access to opportunities and resources for people who might otherwise be excluded or marginalised, such as those who have physical or intellectual disabilities and members of other minority groups.

Oxford Dictionary

Inclusion is the human right to access equal opportunities without discrimination, intolerance, or ignorance. We are removing barriers so everyone can participate equally, independently, and confidently.

Every child has the right to an education according to the Equality Act 2010.

Under the Equality Act 2010, it is unlawful for any education provider, including a private or independent provider, to discriminate between pupils on grounds of disability, race, sex, gender reassignment, pregnancy and maternity, religion or belief, or sex. Discrimination on these grounds (known as "protected characteristics") is unlawful regarding prospective pupils (admissions arrangements), pupils at the school including absent or temporarily excluded pupils, and former pupils who have a continuing relationship with the school. CSIE - Equality Act 2010 www.csie.org.uk/inclusion/equality-act-2010

In this Act, the law must make allowances to accommodate differences with all disabilities. 'Reasonable Adjustments' allow a child to learn to the best of their ability without discrimination.

What is a Reasonable Adjustment?

The Equality Law believes that changing a few elements of an organisation or the environment a person lives in can allow a person not to be disabled. Restructuring or changing the way things are, can enable everyone to achieve. It's about removing barriers.

What is a Reasonable Adjustment Under the Equality Act?

Equality law recognises that achieving equality for disabled people may mean changing the way that employment is structured. This could be removing physical barriers or providing extra support for a disabled worker or job applicant.

Equality and Human Rights Commission - Employment/Workplace Adjustments

https://www.equalityhumanrights.com/en/multipage-guide/employment-workplace-adjustments
https://www.equalityhumanrights.com/en/multipage-guide/employment-workplace-adjustments

Right to Education

International human rights law guarantees the right to education. The Universal Declaration on Human Rights, adopted in 1948, proclaims in its article 26: "Everyone has the right to education."
http://www.un.org/en/documents/udhr/index.shtml

Education as a human right means:

- The right to education is guaranteed legally for all without any discrimination
- States have the obligation to protect, respect, and fulfil the right to education
- There are ways to hold States accountable for violations or deprivations of the right to education.

What Guarantees Education as a Right?

The universality of the right to education has been reaffirmed in other treaties covering specific groups, such as for women and girls, persons with disabilities, migrants, refugees, indigenous people, and those who may face other forms of discrimination, as well as in conflict zones. It has also been incorporated into various regional treaties and enshrined as a right in the vast majority of national constitutions.

right-to-education.org

https://www.ohchr.org/en/professionalinterest/pages/cedaw.aspx

https://www.un.org/development/desa/disabilities/convention-on-the-rights-of-persons-with-disabilities.html

https://www.right-to-education.org/resource/status-right-education-migrants-international-legal-framework-remaining-barriers-national

https://www.ohchr.org/en/professionalinterest/pages/crc.aspx

https://www.un.org/development/desa/indigenouspeoples/wp-content/uploads/sites/19/2018/11/UNDRIP_E_web.pdf

https://www.ohchr.org/en/professionalinterest/pages/cerd.aspx

https://www.right-to-education.org/sites/right-to-education.org/files/resource-attachments/RTE_International_Instruments_Right_to_Education_2014.pdf

Why is the Right to Education Fundamental?

Both individuals and society benefit from the right to education. It is fundamental for human, social, and economic development and a key element in achieving lasting peace and sustainable development. It is a powerful tool in developing the full potential of everyone and in promoting individual and collective well-being.

In brief:
- It is an empowerment right
- It lifts marginalised groups out of poverty

- It is an indispensable means of realising other rights
- It contributes to the full development of the human personality. (Inter-Agency Network)

What is Inclusion?

Inclusion in Education - The Warnock Committee

Equality Act 2010: Guidance

The provisions of the Equality Act which came into force on 1 October 2010:

- The basic framework of protection against direct and indirect discrimination, harassment, and victimisation in services and public functions, work, education, associations, and transport
- Changing the definition of gender reassignment by removing the requirement for medical supervision
- Providing protection for people discriminated against because they are perceived to have, or are associated with someone who has, a protected characteristic
- Clearer protection for breastfeeding mothers
- Applying a uniform definition of indirect discrimination to all protected characteristics

Harmonising provisions allowing voluntary positive action

Provisions Relating to Disability

- Extending protection against indirect discrimination to disability
- Introducing the concept of "discrimination arising from disability" to replace protection under previous legislation lost as a result of a legal judgment
- Applying the detriment model to victimisation protection (aligning with the approach in employment law)

- Harmonising the thresholds for the duty to make reasonable adjustments for disabled people
- Extending protection against harassment of employees by third parties to all protected characteristics
- Making it more difficult for disabled people to be unfairly screened out when applying for jobs by restricting the circumstances in which employers can ask job applicants questions about disability or health

From: Government Equalities Office and Equality and Human Rights Commission

Published 27 February 2013

Equality Act 2010 Guidance

Inclusion

The opposite of inclusion is segregation.

In 1948, the Universal Declaration of Human Rights (UDHR) was established. This landmark document, with its 30 articles covering basic dignity and liberty, including the right to education, laid the foundation for the rights of individuals with disabilities. It prohibited discrimination and segregation and emphasised the importance of equal opportunities for all, including those with special needs.

Before the war, the idea of 'Eugenics' became popular. The Germans pursued this with the Jews. In the 'T4 Aktion Program' or the 'T4 Euthanasia Program', disabled individuals and those with learning difficulties were killed, and 300,000 were murdered in a bid to make their race pure. The 'T4 Aktion Program' was a systematic and brutal campaign that targeted individuals with disabilities, leading to the deaths of thousands. This tragic chapter in history underscores the long-standing discrimination and segregation faced by the disabled community.

In 1954, a U.S. Supreme Court landmark case, *Brown v The Education Board*, marked a significant milestone in the fight against segregation in schools. The verdict was that it was unconstitutional to have separate schools for white and African American students. An African American student had to go to the next town to attend school, not her local college. The 14th Amendment concerning the 'Equal Protection' clause was enacted. The 'Separate but equal' doctrine did not work as the inequality in the education system made African American students feel inferior. The *Brown v Education Board* case was a turning point in the battle for equal rights in education, paving the way for further progress in inclusive education and disability rights.

African Americans felt support from the courts, and many Civil Rights movements grew. The Civil Rights movement in the 1960s showed many minority groups that they could ask for equal citizenship. In 1971, 14 students with disabilities used the *Brown v Education Board* verdict and the 14th Amendment to win a case allowing them to be educated in a mainstream school.

In England

Education Act 1960

This Act created 11 categories of impairment, and thousands of disabled children were placed in 'junior centres' and institutions.

- *Children and Young Persons Act 1969*

The Local Education Authority (LEA) was made responsible for children not receiving education or those needing care or control.

- *Education (Handicapped Children) Act 1970* and *The Chronically Sick and Disabled Persons Act 1971*

These Acts transferred the education of severely disabled children (previously called "Handicapped") from hospitals to the Local Education Authority (LEA). The latter Act pressed the LEA to improve services for disabled people.

The Beginning of the Disability Anti-Discriminatory Movement

The Disability Movement began following a letter in *The Guardian* by Paul Wade, which helped bring together the Disability Movement to fight against discrimination.

Over the years, charities, foundations, and associations have formed to support disabled and mental health causes, which brought disabled people onto the streets and made the issues visible.

- *1975: UPIAS - Union of the Physically Impaired Against Segregation*

UPIAS argued that the world favours those who fit in — the non-disabled people — and excludes those who are disabled.

Warnock Committee Report in 1978

This committee investigated the education of children and young people in light of public unrest concerning the Disability Movement and the handing over of services from hospitals to Local Education Authorities. Institutions and asylums were deemed outdated and needed to integrate disabled people into appropriate employment, which meant educating them. The inquiry aimed to eliminate differences in education between students with and without disabilities.

The Secretary of State for Education in 1973, Margaret Thatcher, along with her counterparts in Scotland and Wales, and the Secretary of State for Social Services and Employment, appointed Mary Warnock as Chairperson.

Areas they looked at:

- The needs of handicapped children under 5
- Education of handicapped children in ordinary schools
- Day special schools and boarding provision
- The educational and other needs of school leavers

The summary of recommendations included 220 items for the implementation of support and education for those with special educational needs in mainstream and special schools.

Warnock Report

Many of the recommendations are still valid. One recommendation was that initial teacher training must include a mandatory unit to prepare teachers to teach children with disabilities, which was included in teacher training in 2016.

The UNESCO Salamanca Statement on Special Needs Education

In 1994, the international community developed a framework for inclusive education and raised awareness, as more children with disabilities wanted to access their local schools. Many countries worldwide have updated their policies and procedures, with the profile of Special Educational Needs policies and procedures being clearly defined.

The Convention on the Rights of Persons with Disabilities (CRPD)

The CRPD was adopted in 2006 by the United Nations and came into force in 2008. It protects the rights and dignity of those with disabilities, focusing on autonomy, non-discrimination, participation, inclusion, equal opportunity, and accessibility.

Article 24 of the CRPD - Education explicitly states the right to inclusive education.

Ten years later, in 2016, the United Nations, via the CRPD Committee, further defined inclusion in education in Article 24, stating the right to an education and the steps to achieve it.

In England

Every Child Matters - 'Green Paper' in 2003

Following the death of Victoria Climbié, whom the services failed to protect, a 'Green Paper' set out by the Government delivered a proposal to reform childcare. Services were not working together to share information about vulnerable children, so schools, social care, and Child and Adolescent Mental Health Services (CAMHS) joined forces to share information. There were five aims:

- Be healthy
- Stay safe

- Enjoy and achieve
- Make a positive contribution
- Achieve economic well-being

In 2010, the Coalition Government changed parts of *Every Child Matters* to 'Helping the Children Achieve More'; the focus remained the same, but funding changed.

Special Educational Needs and Disability Act (SENDA) 2004

SENDA extended the protection for disabled young people from discrimination in education in mainstream schools, colleges, and universities.

The Lamb Inquiry in 2009

Lord Lamb's inquiry called for 'a radical overhaul' within a report concerning Special Needs Education and parental confidence. The report addressed the low expectations of children and young people with SEND. There has been a failure to deliver what children and families needed. There needed to be 'greater ambition'. He made 51 recommendations.

Parental Satisfaction: Messages from the Research

Main themes:

- Most parents of children with special educational needs (SEN) are satisfied with their child's current school, whether special or mainstream, and favour the current school over an alternative.
- 85% of parents of children with SEN are satisfied with the current school placement for their child.
- Parents of children with SEN are less satisfied with their child's school placement than parents of children who do not have SEN.

Where studies showed parents were not happy with either a particular aspect of provision or sometimes the overall type of provision, key factors were:
- The extent to which the school, teachers, and support staff understood the nature of their child's disability or learning difficulty.
- The willingness of the school to listen to parents' views and respond flexibly to their child's needs.

Equality Act 2010

Many laws have been created over the last 50 years that cover discrimination. Still, the Equality Act consolidated all these laws by covering what they called nine protected characteristics from discrimination. These are:
- Age
- Disability
- Gender reassignment
- Marriage and civil partnership
- Pregnancy and maternity
- Race
- Religion or belief
- Sex
- Sexual orientation

This Act was more comprehensive, covering the workplace, education, social groups, transport, and other areas.

Children and Families Act 2014

Disability, learning difficulties, and mental health issues are so closely entwined together through history and have not always been included in society. Learning disabilities may have complex needs, and they usually have reduced intellectual abilities needing support with daily living, but you can't disregard people just because they don't fit in.

People with learning difficulties blend into society on the surface, with no visible difference. Their learning difficulty does not affect their intellect, but education and society don't always accept their differences.

There is no reason why an autistic child can't learn how to deal with social situations. Many are not identified early enough and given a chance to learn skills before they go into the adult world. Then, they are vulnerable to exploitation, crime, and mental health issues.

SEND Code of Practice: 0 to 25

This Code introduced the Children and Families Act, which presented changes to the system for children with Special Educational Needs and Disabilities (SEND). Published and maintained by the Department for Education, it covers children from birth to 25 years, from the beginning of childcare to employment. There is an emphasis on coordinated care across education, health, and social services, ensuring that information is shared and everyone knows what is happening with children and young people, especially those at risk. This Code also brings in safeguarding and child protection.

Areas considered by the policy that come under the SEND policy include:

Communication and Interaction

Speech and language and communication needs (SLCN)

Cognition and Learning

Struggling with literacy and numeracy, such as Dyslexia (reading and literacy), Dyspraxia (physical coordination), and Dyscalculia (maths)

Social, Mental, and Emotional Health

Support regulating and managing emotions, Autism Spectrum Disorder (ASD), Attention Deficit Hyperactivity Disorder (ADHD), and anxiety and other mental health issues.

Sensory and Physical Needs

Autism, cerebral palsy, visual and hearing impairment

(These are just labels to help define and understand the different categories.)

The SEND provision must consider the child and the parents' views, wishes, and feelings, putting them at the heart of the care with financial support if needed, in the form of an Education, Health, and Care Plan (EHCP).

Many children don't need an EHCP but can be supported with targeted support in the classroom. Every school is required to appoint a teacher in the senior leadership role who would coordinate the support and education of these children in the school and liaise with outside agencies — Special Educational Needs Coordinator (SENCo).

SEND Code of Practice

The Lasting Legacy of Spending Cuts

Between 2010 and 2019, total public spending on education across the UK fell by £10 billion, or 8%, in real terms. This led to a fall in the share of national income devoted to education spending (down from 5% of national income in 2007 to 4.4% in 2019). If education spending had remained at 5% of national income, it would have been £16 billion higher in 2019. There was a 3% real-terms increase in education spending in 2020, but this mainly reflects the temporary extra levels of support during the pandemic.

Source: Nuffield Foundation

The Impact of the COVID 19 Pandemic.

In 2020, the pandemic forced us to work and undertake home learning. Returning to normal, we can now see the increase in mental health issues and educational gaps that our children have. It is not wholly the fault of the pandemic, as many problems with literacy and maths have been in the making for years. Mental health issues increased during lockdown for many reasons, but they have been on the rise over the last few decades. There has been a lack of funding and priority for child and adolescent mental health services and mental health support overall.

Families' Experience of the SEND System at the Start of 2020

Over five years after the Code of Practice was published, Ofsted's Annual Report 2019/20 concluded that 'in many cases, the goal of creating a child-centred system is not being fully met'. Frustration and misunderstanding were commonplace in many parents' experiences. Many felt that the system was simply not helping their children well enough to achieve their goals. The last 10 years had done little to ease the need for 'warrior parents'.

Parents still felt that they had to 'fight for the rights' of their children. Indeed, in many cases, parents felt that they were rarely taken seriously. They said that when opportunities were provided for them to contribute, they were often ignored. The comment below, made by a parent in one of our area SEND inspections, is similar to the views of many:

"Even if you are 'lucky' enough to get an EHCP, it is usually not worth the paper it is written on! They are written so poorly and the support is never specified or quantified, despite the professionals' recommended services and/or therapies. The parent's voice is usually not heard."

Many parents who expressed their views in successive SEND inspections felt that once they had secured an EHC plan for their child, the struggle was far from over. Many felt that they were the only ones bringing the plan together. They reported having to regularly update other services on what professionals from other agencies were doing:

"They do not work together at all. It's a constant fight to get them to talk to each other or to work together on a plan that might help our son."

www.gov.uk/government/publications/send-old-issues-new-issues-next-steps/send-old-issues-new-issues-next-steps#send-the-recent-pas

The Government's Green Paper 2022 was about reforming SEND and discusses the vicious cycle of late intervention, low confidence, and inefficient resource allocation. They talk about the large amounts of money spent on EHCPs and the need for a better system. Many children need support, and their cases require financial and special consideration.

www.gov.uk/government/publications/send-and-ap-green-paper-responding-to-the-consultation/summary-of-the- send-review- right-support-right- place-right-time)

Chapter 10

The SENCo

What is a SENCo?

The Special Educational Needs Co-ordinator (SENCo) plays a crucial role in our education system. They are responsible for identifying and providing support to all children in the school who require extra assistance due to special needs. This person, who is often a teacher or headteacher, is a key figure in ensuring that every child's unique learning needs are met. While not required initially to be qualified, the teacher has three years in the post to qualify as a SENCo, as mandated by law since 2008.

The Government legislation—SEND Code of Practice 0-25 years—states that teachers or headteachers who apply for the post are asked to promise to complete the SENCo course within three years of starting the role if they are not already qualified.

https://www.gov.uk/government/publications/send-code-of-practice-0-to-25

Update on Qualification

In 2024, the National Award in SEN Coordination was replaced with a leadership-level national professional qualification (NPQ). The government amended The Special Educational Needs and Disability Regulations 2024 to introduce the NPQ as the mandatory SENCo qualification from 1 September 2024.

https://www.gov.uk/government/publications/mandatory-qualification-for-sencos/transition-to-national-professional-qualification-for-special-educational-needs-co-ordinators

The Roles of a SENCo

- To identify children in the school with Special Educational Needs and Disabilities (SEND)

- To develop and oversee the school SEND strategy
- To design and deliver care and interventions to support the child in the school and reduce the attainment gap if necessary
- To assess and monitor the progress of SEN pupils
- To liaise with other care professionals, health, and social care, along with the headteacher and class teacher
- To support teachers in developing and implementing learning plans and behavioural support
- To manage and collaborate with other agencies on the SEND budget

The SEND Code of Practice

The SEND Code of Practice is a piece of government legislation that provides guidance on the Special Educational Needs and Disability (SEND) system for children and young people aged 0 to 25 from 1 September. This was developed from The Children and Families Act 2014, which set out key principles:

- Children, young people, and their families or carers will be central to decision-making in the care they are given. This is called co-production.
- Health, education, and social care will work together rather than as separate entities.
- The care will identify needs early on and continue through until the child is 25 years old.

A report came out on 16th June 2021 from Ofsted, titled *Research and Analysis - SEND: Old Issues, New Issues, Next Steps*. Following Ofsted inspections from the introduction of this policy in 2016 to 2020, many areas of the country struggled with the implementation of this policy, due to:

- Lack of joined-up care between health, education, and social care
- No co-production, or poor co-production
- Poor quality of Education, Health, and Care Plans (EHCPs)

Special needs education covers every child because every child learns uniquely. Most children with special needs, and those with extra learning needs such as dyslexia and high-functioning autism, are in mainstream schools, working alongside children with no apparent needs. I say 'apparent needs' because every child learns differently, so every child has some learning needs. I believe every teacher needs a better understanding of special needs because every child has a bit of autism or ADHD, dyslexia, dyspraxia, or dyscalculia. We are all on a spectrum because we are all human.

Spotting children early and providing support can reduce the risk of mental health issues and improve confidence. Hopefully, these children will have positive outcomes in life, such as believing in themselves. Alternatively, branding them as 'naughty' could lead to poor self-esteem and outcomes such as not reaching their potential, experiencing mental health issues and becoming involved in crime.

Many issues go undetected because there are not enough qualified and experienced SENCo staff. The knock-on effect is that children who struggle in class or the classroom environment, are seen as disruptive, or fail to reach their potential because they need help processing information. Schools cannot afford to ask why.

Workload

Each school usually has only one SENCo, so their workload is huge, covering legal implications, safeguarding, pastoral care, mental health and tribunals. Also, there is ongoing support for those already with Education, Health and Care Plans (EHCPs) and the regular care of pupils with special educational needs. This is a challenging role in schools, especially with the funding constraints they face. Teachers usually pick up on a child's struggle with learning or in their interaction with their peers. A small primary school could have 300 pupils, and a secondary school could have more than 2,500 pupils. Some SENCo staff are part-time or have a dual role as headteachers.

Safeguarding

Safeguarding implications are also relevant for these children, who can go unnoticed in school. Some feel it's their fault that they can't sit down and work like other children. Autistic children need to be considered as 'vulnerable children' due to their lack of understanding of social situations. How many children are falling through the system because, as Ofsted said, SENCos are unable to identify or assess children with special or extra needs? When a parent asks for help and behaviour is not observed in school, it can be challenging to convince staff otherwise. With little knowledge and understanding, staff may neglect the very role they have been appointed to undertake.

How many children are being repeatedly punished and sent out of class due to their behaviour, when what is really happening is that many have some learning difficulties and lose their motivation to learn? As they see it, they no longer believe they can achieve their dreams, so they might as well have some fun.

If a school identifies an issue, it has a 'duty' to support that pupil, but it seems as though they want to avoid actively looking because they will need to find the funding. One SENCo in a secondary school said they would only refer for an autism assessment if they saw the presence of mental health issues. Isn't that too late?

Many SENCos have experience with special needs children, either because they have a special needs child at home or because they have worked in a special needs school. However, having an interest is not enough to understand. It took me time to recognise different needs under the guidance of good SENCos, while working as a teaching assistant and observing my son. This continuous learning and development is crucial for all educators to better understand and support children with special needs

Children with profound special needs and disabilities are looked after because their issues are more visible, such as being in a wheelchair, being obviously hearing impaired, or requiring medical feeding. Many children try very hard to hide their differences to be accepted by their peers – 'masking' – but this usually backfires and they don't receive the support they need.

I phoned on many occasions to ask for support from the SENCo for my son's dyspraxia and there was also a question about autism while I was waiting for an assessment. They didn't seem to understand what I was saying. He only needed to sit near the teacher to hear the lesson above the class noise. He also needed some critical points of the lesson as a reminder, as he struggled with processing information and could miss key details. Everything was so vague. There needed to be more creativity and flexibility in how they perceived support. They immediately thought I was asking for a one-to-one, but that would have been his worst nightmare and was not needed as he understood how he learned best.

Staff Education is Needed

More information and education are required. There needs to be more consistency. Many Academies are pushing through the curriculum without considering educational differences and Special Educational Needs. How can inclusion be taken seriously when a teacher thinks it's okay for an 8-year-old autistic child to be calmed down by sitting in a box in the classroom? It just creates another reason for other children to laugh at them. So much of the support that's implemented for children with neurodiverse needs is based on stereotypes of what teachers and educators think neurodiverse children need.

As my child would say, 'You don't know my Autism'.

Sixth Form

Some sixth forms don't have SENCo cover. Why is this? Is there an assumption that there will be no special needs students in sixth form? Is it because people think that autism, ADHD, and specific learning difficulties prevent students from doing A levels or retakes?

Many children with neurodiversity are clever.

None of these special educational needs affect a person's intelligence; they just have a different way of learning. The education system makes them appear unintelligent because schools struggle to accommodate their differences, making it difficult for them to achieve. The education system is about fitting children into the academies curriculum.

You are only as good as the support around you.

Some fantastic teachers know their students and how to adapt and support their teaching. But what happens when the child gets behind with their work or becomes disruptive? A teacher has 30 children to help, so the lesson stops; the teacher has to ensure the child is safe or calm. If a Learning Support Assistant is in the classroom, the learning doesn't stop, and someone can look after the child. Funding under the Academy system cuts back on classroom support when money needs to be saved. Too much work is put on one teacher in a class of 30 pupils. Classroom support makes their job so much more effective and enjoyable.

A SENCo needs to rely on the teacher to inform them if they have children in their class who are struggling academically or behaviourally. A teacher needs to see the behaviour as a concern, not an inconvenience, and not simply send the child out of the class.

Teaching Assistants are sometimes not qualified for their role, often after having been a school dinner lady or helping out in another capacity at school.

If you don't have experience of knowing what an autistic child looks like, you won't understand their behaviour when they are distressed. Their world is falling apart, and they are trying very hard to fit in; they are masking with immense anxiety.

That child with ADHD who can't stop moving today is not being naughty!

Spotting children early and providing support can reduce the risk of mental health issues and can improve confidence. Hopefully, these children will have positive outcomes in life, such as believing in themselves. Alternatively, they may be branded as naughty, leaving school with less than they were capable of, with poor self-esteem—outcomes such as not reaching their potential and happiness in life, mental health issues and even possibly crime.

When they leave school, it's not the school's problem. Once a child is 21, the school is no longer legally responsible for anything that happened at school. But have they incubated this? Traumatic events in our childhood will affect the rest of our lives if we cannot resolve the issues.

Chapter 11

Academies

If you want a diverse workforce don't educate children as though they are clones.

Why are so many teachers getting disillusioned with teaching and leaving the profession?

Children spend a lot of their waking time at school; why is childhood mental health on the rise?

You can't blame it *all* on Covid.

Education is the kindling of the flame, not the filling of a vessel – Socrates.

What are Academies?

An Academy is a state-funded school that the Government funds directly. Before this, the Local Education Authority managed the schools, which were accountable to and funded by the government. The National School Board was formed in 1909, as local authorities had different land and financial boundaries.

The change to Academies brought more freedom and autonomy to schools, removing a layer of bureaucracy. More money came to the schools – so they said. The plan is for many schools to come together as Multi-Academy Trusts to share the sourcing of services and get the best value for money, as it would be utilised by many schools at once. The Trusts could set the wages for teachers and other professionals, getting the best for their pupils and carrying out long-awaited building repairs.

What is the board of trustees but a layer of bureaucracy between the schools and the government?

Three types of Academies

- **Converters**: Formerly council-run schools that become part of an Academy Trust.

- **Sponsored**: Previously council-run schools judged by Ofsted to be underperforming had to join a Multi-Academy Trust for support.
- **Free Schools**: A type of Academy not run by any local education board but funded by the government. Parents and teachers have more control over how the school is managed.

Multi-academy trusts are charities and are companies limited by guarantee, so the trustees are company directors. Unlike other charities, schools and academic establishments such as colleges and universities have trustees who are governors on a board.

'The Academies Act 2010 makes significant changes to the framework for academies. It deems that all academies approved by the Secretary of State are automatically charities and that all existing academies became exempt charities when the Secretary of State for Education became their Principal Regulator.'

https://www.gov.uk/government/publications/regulation-of-schools-and-academies-with-exempt-charity-status

Monitoring Schools

Ofsted continues to assess and share accountability with the Multi-Academy Trusts to produce the best education for their pupils. The government decided that a school rated 'Excellent' didn't need routine checks, but this has meant that many schools have gone for too long without inspection. Many processes have changed since COVID-19.

The Academy must follow an evidence-based curriculum delivered to teachers. A curriculum is usually designed and given to all the schools in the trust, regardless of the type of school, location, or relevance to pupils.

While the Multi-Academy Trust has eliminated a tier between the schools and the Academy head, it has introduced another department or layer.

The Department for National and Regional School Commissioners works in their own region to improve the outcomes of children's education, social care and SEND. They work on behalf of the Secretary of State for Education. Regional directors' primary responsibilities include:

- Addressing underperformance in schools, academies, children's social care, and special educational needs and disabilities (SEND) services, offering support, and, where necessary, intervening to deliver rapid improvement
- Taking decisions on academy sponsor matches and significant changes to academies
- Deciding on new free schools
- Taking decisions on the creation, consolidation, and growth of multi-academy trusts (MATs)
- Supporting local authorities to ensure that every local area has sufficient places for pupils
- Delivering across several key programmes by building the department's presence locally through working closely with stakeholders, local authorities, MATs, Ofsted, and other local government departments
- Making sure local needs inform policy development
- Leading the response to area-wide special educational needs (SEN) inspections, ensuring effective challenge and support to enable areas of weakness to be remedied quickly
- Taking the lead on safeguarding cases in their region
- Promoting financial health in the academy trusts and free schools sectors
- Leading on non-financial governance and safeguarding in their region
- Delivering across a number of key programmes emerging from the schools white paper, the SEND and AP green paper, and from the care review

www.gov.uk/government/organisations/regional-department-for-education-dfe-directors/about

The regional Schools Commissioners work with the Education and Skills Funding Agency (ESFA) to provide educational funding for children, young people, and adults. They also monitor Academies, ensuring they work within the Academy guidelines and support failing trusts.

The Education and Skills Funding Agency publishes a report and accounts for 2021-2022.

https://www.gov.uk/government/news/esfa-publishes-annual-report-and-accounts-for-2021-to-2022

While regional school administrators are seen as a good thing, overseeing the progress of the Academies and Free Schools, it is widely accepted that the government needs to manage the increasing growth of Academies directly.

In December, in a written answer to the House of Commons Public Accounts Committee, the DfE's permanent secretary Chris Wormald gave the estimated running costs for the RSCs and their offices for the first year as £4.5 million.

https://schoolsweek.co.uk/regional-school-commissioner-pay-revealed/

Effectiveness of Academies

I will leave the effectiveness of Academies to the researchers, as they can choose the information they want to present from the research they gather. Many successful schools in Multi-Academy Trusts are riding on good Ofsted assessments that have not been checked for up to 10 years. Head of Ofsted Amanda Spielman in 2019 stated that assessments of schools only give half the view of what is going on in our education system. Since Covid, more schools that were graded as Outstanding have been inspected.

https://www.theguardian.com/education/2019/jul/15/head-of-ofsted-calls-for-greater-scrutiny-of-multi-academy-trusts

Advantages and Disadvantages of Academies
Advantages:

- Groups of schools can work together on curriculums and share research and expertise.
- Manage their own budgets.
- Source the best price for services for many schools within a trust.
- Financial regulation by the Government means greater accountability than council-run schools.

Disadvantages:

- It's seen as a 'flagship' for privatisation, bringing market forces into schools.
- Sky-high salaries for the executives of Multi-Academy Trusts.
- The average teaching staff salary is lower than that of council-run schools.
- Academies have reduced the voice of the community, staff, and parents.
- Undermine professional autonomy with standardised teaching methods.
- Excessive accountability and inspection via learning walks, book checks, and constant teacher observations fuel increased workload, forcing teachers out of the profession.

Academies have control and power over the children and the running of the schools. Their directives tie the hands of the teachers on matters such as the SEN register.

Classroom Support

Many teaching assistants do invaluable work supporting children. They can make a difference when a child feels lost in a lesson, during playtime, or when a child walks into the classroom with home concerns. So many deserve training and the knowledge to do an even better job. Children often get told off for misbehaving because the adult cannot identify the child's needs. A child who is autistic may need some time out or may become overstimulated by the noise of the classroom, sometimes seen as misbehaving. Simple adjustments can be made to allow children to participate, and that's what inclusion is. Teaching assistants must be trained to identify and support all the children in the class, but many don't have the necessary skills.

It took the Diploma in Special Needs and work experience in a special school for me to identify the children's different needs, with the support of some excellent teachers and SENCos. I was in a position to have a dialogue with the secondary school SENCo in Year 7 when I identified that my son had some autistic tendencies.

The teaching assistant role has such potential but needs to be valued by the academies. Unfortunately, the roles are cut back to save money.

Supporting any child and giving them support when they don't understand what's happening in their world, profoundly impacts their confidence and well-being.

A child might sit in a classroom amongst his or her peers, feeling like they are the only one who doesn't understand and then they go out into the playground feeling sad. The teacher tells the child off for not concentrating, but the truth is that they can't process the information given in the way that the lesson is being taught. Then someone comes over to help.

It may take some time for a teacher to understand that a child is struggling and some teachers may never see it.

Looking after people is about more than just following instructions. Many teaching assistants are dinner ladies or mums who see this role as fitting in with their children's lives. Dealing with issues of confidentiality and safeguarding are serious, so employment needs to be carefully considered. The Academy must value teaching assistants by training them to do what is required.

Many teaching assistants may have never seen an autistic child or understand that a child with ADHD needs to move while they learn. It's easy to tell a child off for not listening or not doing their work, but it takes insight to understand why. I understood the difference between a child at home and a child at school but in our case, the school didn't get it. Don't we mask our behaviour in different situations, if we feel we will be laughed at or have something to hide? We do, it's human nature.

They still haven't helped those with Special Educational Needs who don't need statements and this probably covers many unidentified children in every class. When the government produces a White Paper or a Green Paper about Special Educational Needs, it just means more money is spent on creating another system within a system to patch up what is not working.

For the Future

As adults, we are responsible for creating caring, inclusive and resilient children. Each generation of children grows faster than the one before and we miss much from their education. Children don't have the community links and support the last generation did when they used to say, 'It takes a village to raise a child.'

Mabel Green

Chapter 12

You Are Going To Struggle With This

I walked into the Year One classroom at my son's primary school on the first day back from the summer holidays. I had not anticipated there would be desks and chairs for each child. In Reception, there were areas of play so the children could go from one activity to another, and they sat on the carpet. Children could walk around and choose what they wanted to do. I instantly thought, "You are going to struggle with this."

I didn't know exactly why I thought my son needed support, but from my five years of experience living with him, it just felt uncomfortable. As a mum, you have a unique insight into how your children work. I decided to be at home with my children, and we spent hours playing and making things. I could see many characteristics that made me feel strongly that he would struggle. He did things at his pace, which was fine in our 'home world'. I was beginning to see that he was a bit different when playing with others and reflected on how he was in the baby groups and coffee mornings. We had our ways of communicating and sign language, so we managed, but starting preschool, the differences were getting more significant.

I saw a health visitor when my son was five days old and I didn't meet her again until I requested help when my son started preschool. The assessments at 2 and 3 years old were paper questionnaires from the GP. I always knew his vocabulary was limited compared to others, but he understood so much more, so I believed he would catch up; there was so much going on at home with friends and extended family. Those who knew were used to him and he could always make himself understood. The issues came when he started socialising with more children.

My Son

My son's physical development was slower than that of his antenatal peers, but I accepted that he would do things at his own pace. He was happy sitting there sucking his fingers because he used 'sign language' with me and watched what was going on. I knew he understood more than he communicated verbally. We went to baby groups to meet up with friends, but he hated that. If I walked away to get myself a drink, he would scream. He would sit still while the children crawled over him, taking the toys from him. He just watched, sucking his fingers.

He Wanted to Learn

My son always wanted to learn and would ask me to read to him. I remember him saying it was why he wanted to attend school. He would pace up and down the kitchen floor as I read. I remember wondering if he listened to me, but he was happy. One day, when he was pacing up and down, his dad came through the door from work. My son repeated word for word what I had said. It dawned on me that moving around was what he needed to do to help process what he was hearing. Throughout his schooling, I would know if he was doing his homework and by listening to him pacing around his room and talking to himself. My son and I both speak and pace around the house when we are sorting things out in our heads, to the amusement of the rest of the family.

At Primary School

I remember picking up my daughter from the nursery on many occasions. I would see my son walking around the perimeter of the playground, mumbling to himself. He'd had a good lesson and was now processing it, but the children in his class were starting to laugh at him. When a lack of understanding and tolerance of differences appears, sadness comes. The school didn't understand why my son needed to walk around and he could not see what the other children were doing, laughing at him. My son could not help it. It was what he needed to do.

The G.P.

When my son was five years old, I tried to get support via my GP, but all he offered me was parenting skills; he had never met my son.

The primary school brought in an Educational Psychologist to observe my son in the classroom but not in the playground and they didn't believe there was anything to be concerned about. Privately we found that he was dyspraxic, during Year 2, but it took a year for the school to understand what that meant. He would sit at the back of the class with the 'naughty boys' as he called them; he couldn't hear or see much and found it quite stressful.

We had a big tick chart at the bottom of the stairs at home with everything he needed to do to prepare for school. This chart was a visual aid that helped him remember and organise his tasks as he struggled to process more than one thing at a time. His hearing was good, but he couldn't process more than one thing at a time. The chart helped him organise himself.

By Year 3 (7 years old), he says he did his best to hide everything different about himself. When he became overstimulated due to visual triggers or anxious, he struggled to keep a lid on behaviour such as flapping his hands or pacing. The rest of the class were amused and poked fun; they knew how to wind him up. He used to say he just wanted to be invisible.

I talked to each teacher regularly, but the taunting carried on when the children saw there would be no repercussions to their behaviour.

Was I the fussy parent, or was I an advocate?

My son would come home saying he was bored, so in Year 4, we did the whole Carol Vorderman 'Maths Factor' programme and I taught him Human Biology. He knew all the bones in the body and how the body worked on a basic level. We built a child-size skeleton with a week-by-week bedtime reading. We decided to take him to the Dyslexic School for one hour a week for English support. He was not dyslexic, but it helped his English as he struggled to write. They worked out that at 9, he had the reading ability of an 11-year-old, but at primary school, they still saw him as a 'low achiever'. He loved going to the Dyslexia school. It was a relaxing break from the school.

Wanting to be Invisible.

My son is a quiet boy who wanted to get on with what he loves, which is learning. and who just wanted to be invisible, but no one allowed him to be.

His primary school identified that he had different ways and labelled them 'quirky' but didn't want to investigate further. At home, he could be himself; we would all be sitting on the sofa, and he would jump up and down for an entire film, especially if it was exciting. He would rest during the commercial breaks, drink and start again.

The problems start when you try to convey this to the teacher. You have an insight into your child that's not believed, because they don't see it. I never let go because you can't, but I found the more you asked, the less they listened.

I went beyond caring what people thought of me at my son's school because I knew there was something my son needed support for, nothing major, but an understanding that would make his life happier and his learning easier. I didn't care; I just knew I needed to find it.

Teaching Assistant Training

Eventually, I gave up on the primary school teachers and obtained my Teaching Assistant qualification to support my son. Being in his school doing the practical part of my course was tricky, but being out in the playground, I understood what my son was saying. The children in his class understood him better than the teachers. They knew how to wind him up. He likes rules, so when they said he could play, they would keep changing the rules to their advantage. They would laugh when he got cross and walked off, but my son was made to feel that he was the one who needed to grow up.

Outside Activities

He tried to have fun in outside school groups, but the same children were there to laugh at him. He tried scouts, which was okay, but other groups were short-lived due to him feeling left out. It's difficult to explain to a sports person or volunteer leader what's going on with the dynamics in his year group or that you think your son has social challenges, when the school doesn't back you up. You are constantly second-guessing yourself because, after all, they are the professionals; they are saying nothing, but it's all happening at home.

Where do the lines begin and end with bullying, being laughed at, or being misunderstood?

Youth groups have an insight into safeguarding but don't have the whole picture. As a parent, if you try to intervene, it usually makes it worse, in my experience. So, in the end, children like my son don't get the opportunities other children have. Inclusion becomes exclusion.

Secondary School

I had hoped that things would get better when my son got to secondary school, but unfortunately, he went with some of the children who had been at primary school with him. They poked fun at him on his first day in front of the new children in their new tutor group. He could not escape it.

I did my Level 3 Teaching Assistant and the Diploma in Special Educational Needs, which enabled me to work in a special needs school for three months. It was enjoyable supporting 15-year-old boys with a variety of neurodiverse conditions. As I did the course, I worked out that my son could be autistic; he was 11 by this time.

I was on the phone to the SENCo at my son's secondary school. She could see some characteristics, did a school-based assessment, and showed that he was academically in the top 25% of his year, not a 'low achiever'; it made sense now. She left a few months later, and nothing happened.

The Classroom

I asked my son how he coped with the learning in class now he was in secondary school. When he was little, he needed to move to file the information he was learning in his brain. If he didn't, it all backed up, and he couldn't take in the next bit of information. He described 'missing information', so it didn't always make sense. When you have nine subjects and homework, you need more time to review what has been missed in each lesson.

No amount of asking would get the school to consider supporting him, even though the SENCo picked up some degree of autism in him when he was in Year 7. The school changed their SENCos many times, so information got lost, it seemed, but it was there. They didn't understand what I was saying. It was like a bad dream. No one was listening.

We went to another GP and managed to get referred to 'SCAMP' (Social Communication and Autism Multidisciplinary Pathway), which was the process needed to assess if he was autistic. My son was 12, and we waited three years, just before his mock GCSEs, to complete the process.

In Year 9, my son came home asking me to help because he worried about his GCSEs. Learning was important; he didn't know what to do, but he wanted to do well. He said he struggled to hear the teacher and get all the work done and found being around some children stressful. We wrote a personal statement so my son could say how anxious he was and worried about some classroom behaviour. We emailed it to the school and were given an appointment to see his head of year. After dealing with a few boys who were picking on my son, nothing else was done.

From this point, he said he gave up most of his learning and concentrated on dealing with friendships and managing the people around him. He admitted to me recently that he started drinking my Sloe Gin at the age of 14 before school, to manage the social side of life there.

Health Practitioner Assessment

I had an assessment done by a health practitioner who came into the school from the SCAMP panel. She observed my son in an art lesson and observed for herself the anxiety my son was experiencing. The art teacher wondered if my son had a 'social communication issue', as on a few occasions, he had watched my son leave the room distressed when he didn't understand what was happening with some of the children in the lesson; this was in Year 9. This backed up my son's concern, expressed earlier that year in his testament to his house head, but still nothing.

I did try to communicate with the school at regular intervals. When it was the school's turn to provide their input for the Autism assessment, they didn't know what to say about my son. When a child is under investigation for Autism, perhaps it would be helpful to speak with the child's subject teachers?

My son came to Secondary school with a diagnosis of Dyspraxia. He sat in their SENCo department for many lunchtimes over 18 months, but it did not occur to them to speak to him to gather information. As a result, they were unable to discuss his concerns and challenges at school. When a teaching assistant attended the Autism Assessment panel, she had little to contribute. We didn't get the statement due to the lack of support from the school.

Mock GCSEs

He got through his mock GCSEs and didn't do much revision, except for Maths. He was in foundation Maths but needed a grade 6 to pursue A-level sciences. He asked to sit the higher Maths exam, and within six weeks, he self-taught the difference in the curriculum and achieved his goal of a grade 6 in both papers. That was unnecessary stress. He still did well in his GCSEs, passing all 10. I often wonder what he could have achieved with support. We went into lockdown, and it seemed like a relief to escape school. He had given up on learning and was glad to be in lockdown.

After Lockdown and Back to School in Sixth Form

The SCAMP panel advised treating him as if he were Autistic and gave him the label of 'Pragmatic Social Communication Difficulties'. The clue in this label is 'Social Difficulties'. The SENCo received all this information, but I heard nothing. Why?

There was no SENCo cover in the sixth form.

My son lost confidence in his abilities, ruining his education and leading him to drop out. He was doing well with his learning but could no longer cope with the stress and anxiety without support from the school.

Adults forget how much of a 'minefield' the social world is when they are teenagers. No one is going to learn if they are unhappy or anxious.

My son wanted to do A-levels, so in response to one of her emails, I replied to the SENCo saying that while his life was calm at home, I sensed his anxieties were rising. I asked if there would be a plan to support him socially so that he could do A-levels. I heard nothing.

There didn't seem to be any SENCo support in the sixth form.

There were children there with Autism and ADHD; where was the support for them?

While he was doing his A-levels, he would come home and review the lessons, which proved effective. He was predicted a B in Biology, a C in Chemistry, and a C in History for his three A-levels. He was doing well after lockdown, but when we went online during the Winter Lockdown, he struggled with interpreting the work, via video. His confidence dropped, but he was still working, covering his bedroom walls with 'mind maps' for his subjects.

The sad part was that he enjoyed his A-levels. He came into his own, worked hard, and his subject teachers were impressed with his grades. The social aspect increased because they were getting older and had more freedom, but this is when it can all fall apart. I spoke to a lovely Pastoral Support Teacher who was helpful but there was no SENCo intervention. He has a diagnosis of Pragmatic Social Communication Disorder, which is a diagnosis given to someone who just misses the threshold for Autism. He struggled to regulate his anxieties with repetitive behaviours which were not seen at school because he had learnt to mask them in order to survive. They didn't believe he engaged in these ritualistic behaviours.

Since leaving, my son has described school as a hostile place.

He would have liked the teachers to have understood how he learns. He struggled with hearing/auditory processing in lessons. He missed so much of the work due to the noise in the classroom. His energy was spent managing his anxieties around some children and their loud behaviour.

He still came out with 10 GCSEs; four were grade 6. He feels he self-taught the most successful subjects at home and believes he could have done better. We don't talk about his A-levels, as he is disappointed that he didn't have the support from the school to finish them.

They took away his right to get an education.

If you don't have a list of qualifications, how will you prove your worth?

Autism is not a mental health issue, but the percentage of those who end up with one is very high. Autism, ADHD, or Dyslexia are labels, and you need good qualifications to get past some people's judgements.

The Future

My son just wanted to learn. When I pass his room, he is always learning something and wanting to discuss it. He is now at home and too clever to be bored, that's when the PTSD and his intrusive thoughts are not playing havoc.

It worries me where my son will end up. His peers and the education system didn't respect him, and now he doesn't want to be a part of society.

Chapter 13

Behaviour

If we teach our children relevant information that they are interested in and if we respect their differences, we will have their attention. Children reach a certain age and realise they fit in, or they don't. We need to validate their skills and talents instead of grading them. We need to prioritise their mental health instead of supporting them when they fall apart with inadequate services. The information they get from social media gives them an outlet but can harm them. For some, what else do they have to validate that they are okay?

The education system could learn a lot from how social media grabs the attention of young teenagers.

We must ask why this is happening because understanding the root causes is the first step towards positive change.

The ABC Behaviour Model Used in Cognitive Behaviour Therapy (CBT)

This framework can help unpick where behaviour comes from. An American psychologist, Albert Ellis, created the model in the 1950s as a precursor to Cognitive Behaviour Therapy (CBT). By returning to the environment or attitudes before the behaviour (the Antecedent), we can identify the reasons for the behaviour by understanding why it is happening. Following the behaviour are usually consequences that have resulted from it. These consequences can produce negative situations or create incentives to continue positive behaviour.

A - Antecedent
B - Behaviour
C - Consequences

Unpicking negative behaviour and understanding why children are disruptive will enable adults to respond to their challenges and modify the environment. We must be more proactive and supportive instead of just dealing with the consequences and giving them detention. Alternatively, children can see that a positive attitude creates positive behaviour and a favourable outcome. So many children struggling at school, who are disruptive or being bullied, are being punished because the teacher is only dealing with the result of a chain of events. A stressed-out autistic child hits out, but why are they stressed?

In this 21st Century

In the 21st Century we are using Victorian teaching methods and attitudes. Some children know what they want to do with their lives and it's very different from what is being offered,. It could be not being able to take the subjects they need at the GCSE level. They are trapped in the system and must prove their worth through these old values and ideas. Teenagers have a better idea of what is happening in the world of technology, and they are going into the future. I usually need a teenager to help me fix a tech problem. Many children are taught subjects with little relevance to their dreams or focus. The Academies are peddling the same system without thought.

Children are trying to learn subjects they are not interested in, and their qualifications are the basis of their future. What they were interested in and what they wanted to be has long gone. Those who don't fit the system nullify their dreams with computer games and drugs or suffer mental health issues.

Useful Skills

- How to look after your mental health
- Executive functioning skills (Listed in Learning Differences)
- Business skills
- Understanding taxes
- Good communication skills
- Good money behaviour with saving and investing
- How to eat healthily and cook

The government would save so much money if we were healthier. In Japan, their diet started to decline with the introduction of the Western diet. They began seeing new chronic illnesses that the Western diet produced. The government recently initiated a plan for every primary school to focus on healthy eating. Every school has a nutritionist who ensures no processed food is served and educates the pupils. Everyone has school meals and the parents support the initiative at home. They all love their broccoli and salads because they understand why they must eat healthily.

In the bigger picture, the food industry would have to see the value in promoting healthier food. Children are given too many options and need more boundaries. Behaviour policies must be consistently applied. There may be so much going on for a child at home that the school has no idea about. We must understand and address these needs.

Instead, they have access to a whole world of information not controlled by anyone via handheld computers and watch the screen instead of where their feet are going.

Who's Agenda Is This?

How would a company work if it is obsessed with the shareholders and the board of directors but shows little regard for the product, workers, or customers?

You get cooperation, motivation, and inspiration if the other party is respected, seen, and valued for who they are, not a product of a system. This respect and value are essential for children and adults in the education system.

Children are in a system that does not aim to understand them. Schools run on an adult agenda. What is worth more in society today?

- A snapshot of a person's intelligence from repeated learning of information
- Or life skills, emotional intelligence, and a motivated lifelong learner with relevant skills

Locking Toilets During Lesson Time

Why do schools lock toilets during teaching time and monitor which children ask to leave the classroom? It doesn't take a behavioural scientist to work out what's going on here. If you don't want to be there, you will find ways of getting out.

Unfortunately, no law stops schools from locking toilets during lessons, but that doesn't mean they should do it! Banning toilet breaks shows a lack of understanding of pupils' health needs and a lack of respect for children.

Source (https://eric.org.uk/information/school-toilet-policy/

The Hydration Equation: Update on Water Balance and Cognitive Performance

Shaun K. Riebl, MS, RD, PhD Student, and Brenda M. Davy, PhD, RD, FACSM, Associate Professor

Water is a crucial nutrient, and hydration is necessary for optimal daily functioning. Water balance is precisely regulated within the body and many methods exist for assessing hydration status. Cognitive performance measures an individual's attentiveness, critical thinking skills, and memory. Traditionally, a 2% or more body water deficit was thought to produce cognitive performance decrements; however, recent literature suggests that even mild dehydration – a body water loss of 1–2% – can impair cognitive performance. Counselling clients about their health and wellbeing should include conveying the importance of water for normal body functioning, as well as its effects on physical and cognitive performance.

http://www.ncbi.nlm.nih.gov/pmc/articles/PMC4207053/
Source

Learning Can Motivate and Inspire

Think about the last time you wanted to learn something, transfixed by the speaker. You feel excited and motivated to learn, and you want to know everything there is to know because you want to get it right. Lost in thought or attention, you have a direction and a purpose.

When a baby learns to crawl and spots a toy just out of reach, they will do all they can to reach it. Children are born learners and are curious about their environment. They learn a lot, independently before they start school. Their personalities show signs of interest and hobbies they may take up. What happens?

What Would Adults Do?

What happens if adults are in a job they cannot get out of, doing work they are not interested in? The outcome could profoundly affect the rest of their lives.

Unfortunately, some 15-year-old children don't see the point of being in school. They sit doing clerical work in subjects they are not interested in and end up being the ones always getting detentions. What's the value of a detention? You are taking them away from the classroom, but they don't want to be there.

One of my son's friends was lively in class but was more interested in the business he was developing and earning from. He was 14 years old. There are sparks of inspiration that didn't fit the school agenda. Think about what this boy could have achieved if he had been encouraged to channel his interests.

There are so many subjects that some children don't need to learn. Do we all need to know about 'longshore drift' in geography? I haven't used trigonometry since 1985.

SATs in Primary School

Teachers need to achieve a specific pass rate for league tables, regardless of the children's ability in their class. Some Academics take the planning away from the teacher and create a generic curriculum that every school must comply with. Constant monitoring and assessment of the teachers ensures that only what the academy wants is taught to ensure that the 'one size fits all' lesson is delivered.

Some children develop their fine motor skills later than others, so they aren't interested in picking up a pen and writing. You can see the girls colouring and the boys outside running around.

At six, my son was not writing enough, but he knew all the names of the bones in the body, how a train engine worked, how a plant made food and he had started reading. He was described as a 'low achiever.'

Success at school can affect the rest of their lives for so many. When you are 18, 14 years of school is a big chunk of your life, especially when you have not felt good enough.

Behaviour in School NASUWT. The Teacher Unions (September 2023)

This report was about concerns of violent and abusive pupils against the teachers in educational settings that are undermining the work they are trying to do. Many teachers don't feel supported and behaviour policies are not correctly implemented. Appropriate people such as parents and other professionals are not always involved. Teachers are there to teach. They are going down the path of least resistance.

If a pupil's behaviour had deteriorated, teachers were asked what they believed was the driving force behind this. They cited:

1. Poor mental health
2. Poor socialisation due to COVID-19 restrictions
3. Lack of proper policies and procedures to deter unacceptable behaviour
4. Lack of training of staff
5. Little or no access to specialist support
6. Lack of support from SMT for classroom teachers
7. Class sizes too big
8. Use of 'restorative behaviour' programmes that are ineffective

The teachers were asked what actions they felt were needed to support them to meet the behaviour needs of all the pupils they teach. They said:

1. More in-class support from teaching assistant, etc
2. More external support - i.e. from child psychologists, CAMHSetc
3. Pupils with behavioural issues being moved into specialist provisions that better meet their needs
4. More Training
5. A curriculum that better meets the needs of and engages pupils
6. More support and assistance from school/college leaders and governors
7. More support and engagement from parents and carers

Restorative conversations

Over half - 56% of the schools used restorative conversations to manage issues between children.

11% said that it was an effective way

36% said they were not sure if it helped

56% said that this was not effective.

https://www.nasuwt.org.uk/static/357990da-90f7-4ca4-b63fc3f781c4d851/Behaviour-in-Schools-Full-Report-September-2023.pdf

If children do not respect the authority, the bullying continues when the adults walk away.

If they are ok at school, it's not an issue at school

Usually, well-behaved children who struggle at school would not 'kick off' because they are too anxious to misbehave at school. They fall apart at home, where they feel safe. Some with conditions such as ADHD, can't help how they act and may have no filter for their behaviour.

Ask the question 'Why' before assuming it's not the school's issue. Some poor behaviour is defined as disruptive, and many children are sent out of class on detention, Referral Units, or 'Off Rolling'.

('Off Rolling' is removing a child from a school, but it is not a permanent exclusion, which benefits the school, not the pupil.)

Understanding behaviour

When I was a teaching assistant, a little boy in my class would get angry and refuse to do his work because he could not calm down. He was told off and sent to the Headteacher to do his work there or during his break time. After watching, I realised that he could not write the date and title down quickly enough, which, in his eyes, messed up the whole lesson for him. I wrote the date and title on a whiteboard to copy when the teacher was taking the register so he was ready for the lesson. From then on, he was happy, and we saw he could do the maths. SENCo was investigating the idea that he could be Autistic.

Some teachers need insight and knowledge into the connection between the school environment and a child's behaviour. Focus should be on more than just giving information to meet a target to achieve a good test result.

I've heard parents say – "At least now that we have got a statement that says our son has ADHD, they can't put him in lots of detentions because of his behaviour in the classroom; they have to support him." That's why many parents get statements because then schools have to look beyond a child's behaviour and support them!

Recent Behavioural Issues highlighted in the media

There is an increase in mental health issues, lockdowns, and poor funding. Children in mainstream schools are exhibiting increased behaviour issues. A School week article stated that schools are losing a quarter of their lessons, having to sort out poor behaviour, affecting other children's and staff's well-being.

(https://schoolsweek.co.uk/schools-lose-a-quarter-of-lesson-time-to-poor-behaviour-dfe-survey/)

Source (https://schoolsweek.co.uk/schools-lose-a-quarter-of-lesson-time-to-poor- behaviour-dfe-survey/)

Chapter 14

What Did Inclusion Mean To My Son?

Inclusion in class meant being identified as different, which led to further ridicule from the other children, so my son preferred to be invisible. Years of being in 'fight or flight' mode every time he walked into a classroom or stood in the playground resulted in PTSD. In sixth form, all they could say was, "What can we do?"

The answer is Nothing; the damage has already been done. Unless you have a time machine, we cannot return to when my son asked for help or when they took me seriously. They probably think he left of his own accord.

When talking to my son, he believes that much of what he learnt in school was self-taught. I wished I had pulled him out of school and home-schooled him, but that was 16 years ago. When I asked the schools to support him, I didn't want a 1-to-1 or extra support. I just wanted them to understand how he learnt so he could achieve. The other children's behaviour made the classroom environment too noisy and stressful. He struggled with their unpredictable behaviour.

He knew what he needed to do. His favourite teacher was one of the strictest primary school teachers, who got the class to work quietly. Listening is harder for him when he sits down because he processes information when he paces up and down. He would have coped with the noise if he could move. Don't we sometimes get our ideas on a walk or process what we think when we move? But we insist that children need to sit and listen.

After the diagnosis of Dyspraxia in Year 2, the teacher didn't know what to do with him, so he was put at the back of the classroom and would come home saying he was bored because he could not hear or see very well. At home, we read weekly publications about human biology, and building a skeleton was our bedtime reading.

At the beginning of Year 4, he came home and said, "The teacher doesn't think I'm very clever." They weren't getting it and this boy deserved an education. So, I did half an hour of maths with him every weekday for almost a year using Carol Vorderman's Maths Factor. For his English, we paid for an hour at the Dyslexia School. He wasn't dyslexic, but they understood the support he needed. At the age of 9, he had a reading age of 11. He reads so much about so many different things. I had to pretend I understood history, science, war, and the politics of Star Wars. He is still reading everything he can get his hands on and has not stopped talking. I even sometimes pretend I understand what he is saying!

It's so hard to watch your son fall apart as he closes the door on the outside world. I could not do anything about it in primary school or secondary school. My son would hold it all in at school or mask it, but as soon as he shut the front door, he would let all the emotions of the day out—crying, anger, or just talking. With all this to manage, he knew he couldn't do what he wanted, which was to learn.

In primary school, the teachers knew my son was honest, so they called upon him to comment on incidents he had observed. That made him more anxious and vulnerable when returning to class because he had put another child in trouble. But they didn't believe him when he expressed his anxieties about being in the classroom with other class members. He was made to feel that he was the problem. As time passed, it was clear the teachers were not interested in what he had to say; nothing was resolved, so it continued.

We had a holiday in Normandy, France, when my son was 10. He was my tour guide as we visited all the beaches. He knew who came over the top, what happened and all the facts and figures. This love of history got him through his GCSE history and onto his History A Level.

Secondary School

My son struggled to hold it together at school, but if he showed anyone that he was upset, that led to more ridicule. He said they had got to him. The children from primary school who had followed him to secondary school knew how to wind him up, and it was always in front of a crowd. He didn't know how to handle it—he is autistic. He said sometimes the only way to stop it was to challenge individuals to a fight, as a good thump would sometimes stop them; he had nothing else, especially as the adults around him were not listening. It's not in his nature to hit out, but he had to defend himself.

He says he gave up on many subjects in secondary school from Year 9 because he sometimes felt so anxious and could not hear the teacher. He started worrying about his work and that he would not do well in his GCSEs. We tried emails and school visits. My son wrote a statement about how he felt and his ongoing issues with some of the boys.

We sent it to one of the school's deputies as we had no luck with the SENCo. I could see year after year his anxiety was getting worse, and we were also in the process of getting an autism assessment. We went into the school, and the head of his house sat with us and read it. Nothing else happened in response to asking for help. At 15, he started drinking my Sloe Gin to manage his increasing anxiety at school, unbeknown to me.

He walked into primary school saying, "I will learn to read," even though he had issues with his speech. He walked into secondary school and said, "I'm going to do triple sciences," and he did, and went on to start Biology and Chemistry at A Level.

I knew this was a very anxious autistic boy, but the school didn't know what they were looking at. The primary issue here is that teachers must know how to identify children with learning difficulties. Many subject teachers in secondary school concentrate on teaching their subject at the expense of understanding how a child is learning. If pupils struggle to process the information the teacher is giving them, the teachers are wasting their time.

As a Parent

You stand in the playground waiting to pick up your child, feeling like an idiot because you must keep going to the teacher to say what you know. Things aren't right - you can see it.

The hardest thing was sending my child to school, knowing that the adults around him didn't believe or take him seriously about what was happening in his world. He felt vulnerable because the other children laughed at his 'different' ways. Not understanding that he had autistic tendencies, the teachers could not see how anxious he was becoming. He was a quiet boy who told me he just wanted to be invisible.

I kept telling him he was starting a new school. The secondary school would be different, with different children, he would make new friends, but many of the children from his primary school, followed him. He wasn't able to make friends or feel safe.

He asked for support by writing to the school, but when nothing happened, he took himself off to the SENCo department to sit on his own during breaks.

In Year 9, the SCAMP process started and finished during the first few months of Year 11. We had an appointment to hear the verdict of all the assessments. The representative from the school, who was supposed to describe how my son managed at school, was a learning support assistant who my son said had not spoken to him about being at school. The professionals on the panel said it was apparent that she had not prepared much information about my son. We were not destined to get the appropriate diagnosis, and subsequently, we had to go through the process again.

Extra Time

Luckily, we were involved with the SCAMP panel when my son was about to do his mock GCSE exams. For some reason, the SENCo decided that my son could have extra time for subjects but not maths and sciences. I can only think that the SENCo thought he was dyslexic, which he's not; he's dyspraxic. A dyspraxic person can have issues across the board with executive functioning. They struggle with planning tasks, working memory and expressing their thoughts clearly. They may need more time to complete a task. This was only partly resolved, and his mocks were his final results after going into lockdown.

Sixth Form

My son started his A Levels doing well as he *could* learn, in his own way, but being in class was too stressful; he had many double lessons that felt too long. He was allowed to leave the classroom, but he would miss the work. I tried contacting the SENCo for support as he started sixth form, but she didn't cover sixth form. He had been through the SCAMP process and was diagnosed with 'Social Pragmatic Communication Disorder' (which is just off the autism spectrum). The panel said he was to be cared for as if he were autistic.

The clue is in the term 'Communication Disorder,' so you may struggle in the sixth form common room with extra free time. To make up for it, he would work many hours at home in the evening. He didn't know how to handle this new routine.

I had a lovely pastoral care person at the start of the sixth form, but it didn't seem as if anyone knew what to do. I never heard anything from the SENCo. Returning to upper sixth form, the designated 'safe place' had been used for something else. There was a plan for him, but no one thought to communicate with my son.

He has an academic record below his abilities and does not want to return to education. It's too traumatic; he can't cope with the environment, and he describes his brain as not working properly anymore.

There is a crossover with the lack of inclusion, poor safeguarding, and an increase in mental health issues with any child in school.

Mabel Green

Chapter 15

Childhood Trauma And Mental Health

It is not just a duty but a collective responsibility of all adults in our society to protect and support our children. The effects of childhood trauma are not transient. They can be profound and enduring, shaping the course of a child's entire life. This underscores the urgency of addressing and preventing such trauma.

What are Adverse Childhood Experiences?

Adverse Childhood Experiences (ACEs) are "highly stressful, potentially traumatic events or situations that occur during childhood and adolescence. They can be a single event or prolonged threats to, and breaches of, the young person's safety, security, trust or bodily integrity." (Young Minds, 2018).

Examples of ACEs:

- Physical abuse
- Sexual abuse
- Emotional abuse
- Living with someone who abused drugs
- Living with someone who abused alcohol
- Exposure to domestic violence
- Living with someone who has gone to prison
- Living with someone with a serious mental illness
- Losing a parent through divorce, death, or abandonment

How Common are ACEs?

In a 2014 UK study on ACEs, 47% of people experienced at least one ACE, with 9% of the population having 4+ ACEs (Bellis et al., 2014).

Impact of ACEs

Just like attachment, experiencing ACEs can have an impact on our future physical and mental health, and often, ACEs can be barriers to healthy attachment relationships forming for children. Some of the effects of ACEs on our physical and mental health are:

- An increase in the risk of certain health problems in adulthood, such as cancer and heart disease, as well as increasing the risk of mental health difficulties, violence, and becoming a victim of violence.
- An increase in the risk of mental health problems, such as anxiety, depression, and post-traumatic stress. One in three diagnosed mental health conditions in adulthood directly relate to ACEs.
- The longer an individual experiences an ACE and the more ACEs someone experiences, the greater the impact it will have on their development and their health.

Some of the other things exposure to ACEs can impact are:

- The ability to recognise and manage different emotions.
- The capacity to make and keep healthy friendships and other relationships.
- The ability to manage behaviour in school settings.
- Difficulties coping with emotions safely without causing harm to self or others.

https://mft.nhs.uk/rmch/services/camhs/young-people/adverse-childhood-experiences-aces-and-attachment/

My child had years of humiliation and bullying at the hands of his peers and a lack of school support. How do you start to work out where you fit into society when you don't trust or respect the adults in society? Dealing as well with being autistic. These school years have had such an impact that this trauma will affect the rest of my now adult child's life.

Children have traumatic starts in life, but when they become adults, their choices are theirs. Do those in the education system see the bigger picture? Three years after leaving compulsory education, the education system is no longer responsible for any neglect on their part. Can they see their effect on the children today, making them the adults of tomorrow, or is it just about giving them knowledge and the short-term gratification of looking great on a school league table?

Mental Health

I don't feel I have come into this world as a person people like or value. *(A quote from my son)*

"They have broken me, and I have nothing left to keep me going. The intrusive thoughts, if they could be sorted, would not be enough as I was born with something that is beyond awful (autism) that I cannot live with, and when I tried to live with it, they just broke me."

(A quote from my son)

My son talked a lot about ending his life because he felt that if he died, he could come back as an average person, and life would be easier! He saw autism as a curse.

Autism, ADHD, or any other learning difficulty are not mental health issues. Through ignorance and a lack of inclusivity and acceptance of difference, we create these mental issues in others.

It is a neurological difference in the way different brains work. Many children with mild autism or what the general public understands as high-functioning autism can learn in mainstream schools and employment.

Looking at the history of learning differences and mental health, we can see why they are linked. Many learning differences are manageable for the child; they have taught themselves to talk, walk, and many other skills before school. Restrictive education creates the issues. Many children deemed capable of fitting into mainstream education with learning difficulties need support; *human nature* is on a spectrum.

Labels are only helpful when we need to understand how someone works. We should not be using labels to control people who are different. We all need labels because we are all different.

Everyone has some degree of learning difficulty, and we are all a bit dyslexic, ADHD, or autistic. The medical model has drawn a line to say that some with specific characteristics don't fit into the 'normal' model of being 'normal'.

Mental Health Foundation

Mental health problems among people with a learning disability are often overlooked, underdiagnosed and left untreated due to poor understanding, awareness, and evidence in this area, with symptoms mistakenly attributed to the person's learning disability.

- Data has shown that people with lower intellectual ability had higher rates of symptoms of common mental health problems (25%) compared to those with average (17.2%) or above-average (13.4%) intellectual functioning.
- One study found that 54% of people with a learning disability have a mental health problem.
- Children with learning disabilities are four and a half times more likely to have a mental health problem than children without a learning disability.

https://www.mentalhealth.org.uk/explore-mental-health/statistics/people-learning-disabilities-statistics

- We need to prioritise creating positive mental health instead of picking up the pieces when a child falls apart. It would be more productive and help prevent the destruction in many children's lives.

"Bad men need nothing more to compass their ends than that good men should look on and do nothing."

John Stuart Mill, Inaugural Address Delivered to the University of St Andrews, 1867.

I feel that when adults have the role of safeguarding children but do not investigate bullying, they are as bad as the bullies themselves.

Reception, Where it All Began

It took me almost a whole school year in Reception to get a teacher to take me seriously in dealing with a child bullying my son. A parent stood in the playground and watched me go into the classroom daily to plead with the teacher to sort the issue out. She knew it was happening but refused to back me up. One day, the teacher proudly came to me saying, "I have just asked the child if he was picking on your son and the child said yes." This episode started in September and ended in July.

Why do teachers struggle to stand up to bullying beyond the 'Anti-bullying' week?

My frequent visits to talk to the teacher did nothing for my reputation as a parent. They didn't believe me, and that was a constant theme throughout my journey with my son's education.

When I noticed my son struggled in the classroom in Year 1, 'my card was marked.' I felt they saw me as a fussy parent, and I was asked to go away.

My son was happy at home, but when he went to school from the beginning, he struggled to process what was happening, and the children around him were allowed to laugh at him. It was easier to blame him for being immature than to deal with how the class responded to him.

I know that children are different beings in different situations. I've worked in schools with children I know outside in the community. A boy can cry in front of their parents when the issue is discussed but continue to bully or torment the next day.

As a dinner lady at my children's school, I could see they were winding him up, but I couldn't do anything about it. The children knew I could do nothing about it because I had been to the school too often. The teachers didn't see the issues. The children carry on inside the school and in outside activities.

My son struggled to interpret the social interactions he encountered and much of the time, he was preoccupied with social anxiety. You are playing catch-up as they struggle to read the non-verbal signs that neurotypical children instinctively know.

Social Clubs

Bullying can filter into every part of a child's life, and it's harder to resolve it when the school doesn't see it. It's tough to ensure the happiness and safety of your child in outside activities because they will encounter the same children in the wider community.

Children are vulnerable to mental health issues when they suffer with other children laughing at them. There's a lasting effect on children, especially if they are autistic or are experiencing anxiety. Feeling anxious, singled out and struggling with the school's social interactions make life hard or even scary. Not much learning is happening when you are in this state. A child will either fall apart or mess about. If children are not getting on with their work, they will more than likely be told off for wasting teaching time. What matters to them is that it's no longer for their benefit.

Mental Health Foundation

We take a life-course approach to mental health because good mental health begins in infancy.

- 20% of adolescents may experience a mental health problem in any given year.
- 50% of mental health problems are established by age 14 and 75% by age 24.
- 10% of children and young people (aged 5 to 16 years) have a clinically diagnosable mental problem, yet 70% of children and adolescents who experience mental health problems have not had appropriate interventions at a sufficiently early age.

(https://www.mentalhealth.org.uk/explore-mental-health/statistics/children-young-people-statistics)

I remember one day after school, my son expressed a concern about getting good enough GCSE grades to get into Sixth Form. Emails to the school didn't really work and going in to talk to the SENCo proved a waste of time, so we decided to write a statement of how he felt. It was sent to his House Head, detailing his concerns and how he struggled in class and during break time with the usual characters.

Sixth Form

After fourteen years of asking for support from my son's schools, we were in crisis. He was managing panic attacks in lessons, missing half the work and re-learning it at home. He was managing to maintain his grades, but the thought of taking his sixth-form mock exams was too much. He feared failing them. It didn't need to be that way, as he was doing well.

Being away from school during lockdown and the summer holidays, he relaxed, but at the end of each school break, I would see him start to worry about returning to school.

There was a point when his anxiety changed, two weeks into his Upper Sixth year. He had come back from the summer holiday feeling good and ready to do the best he could. Whatever grades he would get would be a positive thing. Keeping my son in school was really important, as the work was a focus point and he would hopefully feel more positive with supported social contact. Again, the school had made no provision to support him… well, there was, but ten days into the term, nothing had been said to my son and there was no contact from them. He didn't feel safe, and there was nothing in place. They had a duty of care to support him and…

On Saturday, two weeks later, my son hit rock bottom. He was really anxious and distressed. He didn't know what to do with himself, saying there was no point to his life. I called the CAMHS helpline, but they could not offer anything unless someone was about to hurt themselves or were in imminent danger.

I noticed at 9 pm that lots of texts from people I didn't know were popping up on my phone. Then I noticed a police car sitting outside our house. They wanted to check to see if my son was okay after he had sent a distressing text to his friends: "The school didn't care, CAMHS didn't care, and my parents don't understand; there was not much point to my life."

The following day, Sunday, it was all quiet. It was as if there was a different boy in his bedroom. It was eerie. I wanted the shouting boy back. It was as if he had changed. He was angry, saying the school was a hostile place and they didn't care.

He loved to learn. What was he supposed to do now?

What followed over the next six months was complete neglect of himself because, to him, what was the point of his life? It was really worrying because I didn't know how to reach him. He shut everyone out. I gave up my job as a teaching assistant, which I was really sad about, but I felt that I needed to be around the house, so I took lots of cleaning jobs. We all pitched in and supported each other.

Statistics

The Office for National Statistics (ONS) has published new data showing that just 22% of autistic adults are in any kind of employment.

https://shawmind.org/how-mental-health-affects-education/

The Office for National Statistics (ONS) has published new data that shows just 22% of autistic adults are in any kind of employment.

(https://www.ons.gov.uk/peoplepopulationandcommunity/healthandsocialcare/disability/articles/outcomesfordisabledpeopleintheuk/2020)

(https://www.autism.org.uk/what-we-do/news/new-data-on-the-autism-employment-gap)

Chapter 16

A Safe Place And A Parent's Journey

Some schools and the education system have no idea how their impact affects a child who ends up with mental health issues. By the time a child is 21, the education system is off the hook concerning any legal matters. If the academy holds its breath and the young adults don't kill themselves, then the academy is off the hook. The young adult goes into society and must live with it for the rest of their lives.

Schools don't seem to have an understanding of the impact of bullying and lack of support on my son in school and now. As I write this, I know I am not alone in feeling like this.

Situations like this don't just leave the child traumatised, but the whole family, as well. We all see and live it. It can be challenging for siblings to live with a disabled brother or sister, but even worse, to watch the drama play out in front of them. When the schools wake up to the situation and provide support, it's often too little, too late.

My reasons for saying this are:

My son would always say that his anxiety was due to the situation, in his case, the break times and in class. I have to manage my anxiety, but if I go back into those situations, the triggers are always there. That's why he asked for support.

Imagine constantly living in 'flight or fight' mode most days of your school life, knowing the adults around you were not listening. He talked about feeling constantly paranoid around anyone other than his family. Even now, when we say the wrong thing, he blows up, shouting at us. Life can be black and white for an autistic person. As the PTA chairman for three years, I did my Learning Support Assistant training in his primary school, and I could see he looked scared.

I took time off work to find a way of getting him back to school to finish his A levels or get at least one good grade. My son always said he struggled in the Sixth Form Common Room; he didn't get the social stuff. If he had spoken to someone the day before, he wouldn't have remembered if it had gone okay. He was feeling so stressed that he could not process anything. He came out one day asking me to get him out of there.

I didn't understand what had happened that day until six months later, I heard from a friend. Unfortunately, this was to be my son's last day at school. Another boy, who he struggled with in the sixth form, was poking fun at him. As there was no adult support, my son had learned that the only way of stopping these situations was to hit out. My son was very embarrassed about the situation and didn't know how to manage it. This was ten days into the Upper Sixth Form, with no safe place to go, the support plan had not been explained to him, and no SENCo was covering the sixth form.

I didn't know what happened, so I didn't know that my son could not get his head around how he could possibly return to school after that. He had hoped that the school would call and ask where he was, as he legally needed to be there, or the pastoral team would ask how he was, but there was nothing. The school had a duty of care until March of the following year, and this was in September.

That passed me by, as I was just trying to have fun with him so he would be calm enough for me to get him back to school. It was not lost on him. He texted his friends one evening at the end of September, saying that the school and CAMHS didn't care and I didn't understand. He wanted to end his life.

Dark and Angry

It was as if my son changed overnight from this stressed and anxious boy to being quiet and angry. I could no longer get him out of bed or talk to him. He shut down and took to his room. I had an awful feeling that I had lost him, and I could not reach him anymore.

He kept saying that the school had broken him.

He could not see a way to get back to school, he needed support, and in his mind, they no longer cared. There was no reason why he couldn't have got his A levels. His passion is still learning, reading and researching.

I went back to the school just before Christmas because I needed to see if there was any way that he could come back. There just didn't seem to be anything different than before. Still no SENCo support in the sixth form.

My son always wanted to go to school, even if things were bad. He would tough it out. It's what you do, and he was determined to finish his A levels in whatever form they came in.

And at no point did he ever not want to go to school.

I Can't Afford to Cry - A Parent's Journey

I wake up every morning not wanting to speak. If I spoke, I would hear the reality of what is going on in our lives. I can't afford to cry because I need to keep going. Who will pick up the pieces? I'm so tired, as it never seems to be over for parents who have a child/adult with learning difficulties. Support is limited, so you have to deal with situations on your own.

Why didn't just one adult protect him? They sign legal documents to say they must safeguard the children in their care.

I've spent almost twenty years of my life trying to get through to teachers, the headteachers and SENCos saying my son needs support or that he is being bullied, only to be turned away and made to feel a fool.

I was right, all the time and we were left with a mess that could have been avoided if they had only listened to me. I am only a parent; what do I know about my child?

When the education journey is over, we are left to pick up the pieces of our child's life and hope that this now adult will make the right choices with poor mental health and an angry outlook on society. What will he do with an inadequate education that doesn't fit his ability?

I knew my child was being bullied and humiliated in school from the first year. The adults around him didn't believe him, and asking for support was pointless, but we understood what he needed. Parents with 'lived experience' need to be valued instead of being made to feel silly. You end up questioning what you see and what you know about your child. It felt like there was a fine line between getting help and annoying the teacher.

I have even questioned my own sanity. I would go home, regroup, examine the evidence and go back to school pleading with the staff to help or deal with a situation. No matter how annoying I was, I could not let go of this.

Some days, I wonder if it was all real, if all that heartbreak and tears really happened. Then my son says something, and I am transported back. I look at the school photos on the wall and I am reminded how the front door would open, my son would come in, drop his bag, and either cry or get very angry about the day or even the coach ride home. Sometimes, he would hold it all in for months and I would think that things were better, only to find him crying in bed. Then I would feel so guilty that my talk with the teacher or the Headteacher had not worked and nothing had changed since the last tears.

I sit in my home looking at the primary school pictures on the walls, wondering why it went wrong. Sometimes, it feels unreal, as if it didn't happen. Then I see or hear my son, and the memories confirm the mess we are in. What a waste of a person's intelligence and potential. If he had had support from school, he would have achieved his A levels and taken courses that better reflected his intelligence.

If I had been responsible for this mess my son experienced, Social Care, the Police, Education and Healthcare would take me to court, take my son off me or punish me for being neglectful. As an adult in his life, I would be judged unfit to care for him.

Who Takes Responsibility?

When a person turns 21, as I have said, the education system in law is no longer responsible for their actions while that child was at school. How can that be if your childhood sets you up to be the person you will be as an adult? It's so convenient for adults to blame young adults for their behaviour without examining where that behaviour originated. This goes back to the ABC model of behaviour. Undervalued, excluded and not supported, children turn into adults who are unhappy and angry.

I turned on some music in my car to find the CD playing that had been on repeat while driving my son backwards and forwards to lessons in Upper

Sixth Form. It brought back the feeling of not being able to breathe. It's hard to explain what we went through as a family and are still going through. I failed to protect my son from the professionals who were supposed to educate and support him. As a family, we all live with the consequences.

Consequences on the Family

Many parents give up careers and well-paid jobs to support their children when they fall out of the education system. The long-term mental and emotional stress of holding a family together results in relationship breakups. All this goes on outside the educational setting as the parents of a child with learning difficulties work hard to get an education for their child.

I Had a Life

I gave up a lovely job to become a cleaner. At first, I needed to be around to monitor the situation and keep my son safe. I care about the people I clean for, but it's not my favourite job. I don't feel like a carer, as there are no physical needs to support, but it's a full-time job to keep the family together, ensuring everyone is coping. Parents are always left to pick up the pieces.

You Just Need to Move On

People say you need to move on and leave the school experience behind. The child is now a young adult - but we are trying to sort the mess out. I am just one family of hundreds in this country who are expected to 'just move on'.

All this takes its toll on the mental health of the whole family. We no longer sit together to eat a meal due to family members falling out with each other.

Siblings

What about the siblings of children with learning difficulties? Where are they? They stand on the sidelines watching the bullying of their brother or sister in the playground, helpless to do anything. Stable, calm families at home turn into turmoil as another child in the house struggles with mental health issues. The education system is creating the future of our society, but it needs to see beyond its targets and agenda.

So, What Happens Now?

It's the middle of the night, and I can hear my son singing. It's happy singing; it's not like before when he was singing about suicide and self-hatred. I'm listening to hymns. None that I recognise and I am not interested in finding out at 2 am!

I get on with my son, and he wants to talk. Verbalising always helps him process the information he reads, which leads to a discussion. I want to be involved, but it is exhausting because it can take hours out of your day with the many subjects covered. He is allowed to express his opinion like anybody else, of course, but it can cause a lot of friction. With him, there are no opinions, just facts.

I Have No Place in Society

I struggle to describe the anger and stress in this house, and it's only when I am on my own that I feel the difference in the atmosphere - things are calmer. It worries me when he talks about disliking society. He feels let down and not accepted by his peers. Some days, I just don't know what to say or do for the best. I just listen and try to guide him positively if he is willing to listen.

He didn't ask for this.

Radicalisation, Grooming and Crime

Young adults fall prey to the darker side of the internet and are vulnerable to radicalisation or substance abuse. We have a population of young adults who are so vulnerable but have no support.

A person without purpose can end up in trouble, especially if they feel they have been let down by the society they live in. How can you expect a person to fall into line and be what society wants from an adult when they are treated so poorly as a child? If they do fall out of line, the adults conveniently forget that it was the adults who started it all those years ago.

Where is the Accountability?

My son was just one of hundreds of children who are collateral damage from a system that is not working as it should.

Mabel Green

Chapter 17

Leaving Education - Employment And The Pipeline To Prison

Employment discrimination against individuals with autism in the UK is a significant issue. Only twenty per cent of autistic people are employed compared to fifty per cent of disabled people as a whole. Despite legal protections and increasing awareness, many individuals with autism still encounter various forms of discrimination in the workplace and that's if they even get there.

My Experience with Discrimination in the Autistic World

The label of autism in the education system enables your child to get support. Academies are cutting back on general classroom support, so even a neurotypical child will struggle to get help from an extra adult in the classroom. The only support in the classroom will be for those who have an EHCP (Educational Health Care Plan) and you will need to fight for that.

The Law of Employment

Equality Act 2010: This legislation protects individuals from discrimination in the workplace based on disability, which includes autism. It requires employers to make reasonable adjustments to ensure that employees with disabilities are not at a disadvantage. **Reasonable Adjustments**: Employers are legally obligated to provide accommodations that could help autistic employees perform their job effectively. This might include flexible working hours, changes to the work environment, or specific support systems. *Autism Act 2009:*

Focus on Adults: The Autism Act 2009, a groundbreaking piece of legislation, is the first disability-specific law in England, marking a significant step towards improving services for adults with autism.

Strategic Influence: The Act set the stage for the 'Fulfilling and Rewarding Lives' strategy, a beacon of hope later enhanced by the 'Think Autism' strategy.

With their comprehensive guidance, these strategies play a pivotal role in enhancing health, social care, and support services for adults with autism.

Statutory Guidance: The Act underscores the government's commitment to producing statutory guidance for local authorities and NHS bodies on implementing the autism strategy, thereby ensuring that the needs of autistic adults are met.

The Real World of Employment

Reasonable adjustment means that the employer supports an employee to enable them to work and prevent discrimination. Many people with learning difficulties have only been classed as having difficulties because they have been through an education system that does not understand them. Out in the real world, they have skills and unique abilities that are overlooked. If you come to an interview declaring a diagnosis before an employer has seen their abilities, judgment may be made on a person's diagnosis. A person may prefer not to say they are autistic because they want to be judged on their merits. Anxiety during the interview and an inability to judge the social interaction may prevent the person from proving their worth.

Autism Act 2009 – 10 Years On, It's On Hold

Over the last 10 years, the National Autism Society believes not enough has been done. Two out of three autistic people are not getting the basic living support they need. The Autism strategy was updated in 2019 but then delayed until 2021, with action only for one year. As it stands, the government is prioritising the updated version of the 'Autism Strategy', so the Autism Act is on hold.

Employment Stats

The Office of National Statistics (ONS) published data called 'Outcomes for Disabled People in 2020'. This covered topics such as education, employment, housing, and loneliness. 22% of autistic people report having paid work. 75% of adult autistic people still live at home, compared to 16% of disabled adults. Well-being – rates of anxiety in autism are higher than in other disabilities and the general public as a whole.

The New Review to Boost Employment Prospects for Autistic People

A recent review to boost employment prospects for autistic people was published on 2nd April 2023. The Minister for Disabled People, Health and Work, Tom Pursglove MP, said: "We know autistic people can face barriers moving into employment and staying there. This is often due to employers not having the tools to support autistic people or truly understanding the value of a neurodiverse workforce."

People with autism have particularly low employment rates – with fewer than three in 10 in work – but the Buckland Review of Autism Employment, supported by charity Autistica and the Department for Work and Pensions (DWP), aims to change that.

The Pipeline to Prison

Research shows that multiple exclusions of pupils can result in conviction six years earlier than the rest of the population.

Some poor functional skills are associated with exclusions from school; a high proportion of these will have learning differences and will be convicted at a younger age than their peers.

School-to-prison pipelines: Associations between school exclusion, neuro-disability, and age of first conviction in male prisoners Multiple school exclusions were associated with earlier first convictions, with those excluded once, 2–3 times, and 4 or more times being first convicted 3, 5, and 6 years earlier on average than the never-excluded cohort. Of the excluded cohort, 45% were sent to a Pupil Referral Unit (PRU) (a facility for children excluded from mainstream school).

This suggests that being sent to a PRU is associated with earlier first convictions than exclusion alone. Each standard deviation increase in neurodisability (indexed by lower scores on a functional skills screener, used here as a proxy for neuro-disability) was associated with being 0.5 years younger at first conviction.

Hope Kent, Amanda Kirby, Lee Hogarth, George Leckie, Rosie Cornish, Huw Williams December 2023

Source

The Buckland Review of Autism Employment (First published in Feb 2024)

Despite their wish to work, the latest official statistics show that only around 3 in 10 working-age autistic disabled people are in employment, compared with around 5 in 10 for all disabled people and 8 in 10 for non-disabled people.

https://www.gov.uk/government/publications/the-buckland-review-of-autism-employment-report-and-recommendations/the-buckland-review-of-autism-employment-report-and-recommendations

Source

Research into this subject has holes, and insufficient work exists in different ethnic groups. A lack of education interrupted or incomplete education can lead to poorer job prospects and success in life. A youth 'life course' gives a long perspective on their childhood and how it affects their adulthood and future life choices. We just need to read about acute childhood events to see how a child without support is disadvantaged.

The research below says that suspension has an impact on whether a child ends up in prison, but other factors make it very likely, such as:

- Economic/financial hardship in the family
- Divorce and death of a spouse
- Lack of parental support
- Poor school support for achieving their education
- Poor inclusive support for those with neurodiverse challenges
- Bullying

There are reasons behind most poor behaviours or mental health issues.

Schools may not have the resources or knowledge or may not want to support those children, so sending them to a Pupil Referral Unit creates problems. Many children are undiagnosed with ADHD or autism, which may be the reason for their poor behaviour. Neurodiverse children can be vulnerable children. Many bullied autistic children would welcome anybody to be their friend, regardless of the friend's motive. Is part of this 'grooming' when a vulnerable child gets caught up in things he doesn't understand or can't see the bigger picture?

A Parent's Nightmare

I am talking about neurodiverse children who could cope with education and learning in a mainstream school if they had support. Children work hard to fit in until they fall apart.

Exploring the School-to-Prison Pipeline: How School Suspensions Influence Incarceration During Young Adulthood

Paul Hemez, John J. Brent, and Thomas J. Mowen (Published online 31st October 2019)

Overall, this study builds on work documenting the adverse effects of school discipline by situating their effects on youths' life courses. Although existing studies have highlighted that school discipline may be a turning point towards short-term antisocial life outcomes such as arrest (e.g., Mowen & Brent, 2016), this study uncovers that suspensions may incite adverse long-term outcomes extending into adulthood. When interpreted through the life-course perspective, these findings suggest that suspensions may serve as important antisocial turning points that reshape trajectories and usher youth toward incarceration later in life.

(https://www.ncbi.nlm.nih.gov/pmc/articles/PMC8277150/)

Source

But for the Academies, it is out of sight, out of mind.

Mabel Green

Chapter 18

The Times Educational Commission

The Times Education Commission, in 2023, was the first inquiry into the UK's education system from early years to high school. This report was supported by 22 distinguished experts from political parties, education, and business.

Regarding school behaviour, children need to be more involved with their learning. They need to feel more valued for what they can achieve, their talents, and strengths. If an adult did a role in a company that matched their skills, they would thrive. If they feel they are failing or uninterested, this will affect their abilities and outcomes. As a result, many children think they are not good enough and mental health issues can be triggered. They will achieve more when they find a role suited to their strengths and talents.

Why Is This Not Seen in Children When They Are at School?

Children with potentially excellent organisational or problem-solving skills must be valued and encouraged. Many children with mild learning difficulties, exceptional problem-solving skills and creativity never get jobs because they cannot pass their English or maths GCSEs.

Many children need to see the relevance of some subjects; otherwise, they will eventually get fed up with doing them. They are tested too early in Primary schools so the school can shine in the league tables, but for some, it's too early and they are put off from enjoying the subject. Children will soon have to continue to learn Maths until they are 18. How relevant is the maths for the apprenticeship and degrees they are heading for? Is it better to invest in the earlier years and ensure everyone passes their maths GCSE?

Bilingual parents are more successful in teaching their children to learn more than one language. They make it part of their early life when language is learned. Schools formerly started teaching foreign languages at the start of Secondary school and wondered why they are not getting enough children interested. European schools begin teaching English along with their native language in the first year of school.

Going to school is the most significant part of a child's childhood, but the emphasis is almost entirely on academic success.

Times Educational Commission

Some quotes from the Times Educational Commission report describe our present education system. Many successful entrepreneurs have left school early or have poor academic records. Does our education give future employees the skills they need?

Times Education Commission Report 2023

There are many brilliant teachers doing remarkable work. Still, too often, they are achieving their success despite, not because of, a system that has become over-centralised and determined to micro-manage schools. Lord O'Neill of Gatley, the former chairman of Goldman Sachs Asset Management who helped to set up the Northern Powerhouse Partnership as a Treasury minister, said that Whitehall control-freakery was undermining the Prime Minister's ambition to reduce regional inequality. "The Department for Education has a far too centralised national approach to everything," he said. "Levelling up can mean endless things, but ultimately creating opportunity for all is what it has to be about and the education system is hindering that because it's too rigid. It's tragic."

Paul Johnson, the director of the Institute for Fiscal Studies and a Times education commissioner, said that it was depressing how little had changed since he left the department, where he was chief economist until 2004. "Our system sets an awful lot of children up to fail," he said. "We know that the quarter or so of children who leave primary school not reaching the expected level will not reach the expected level at GCSE, and we have no alternative for them. We continue to have a system that works quite well for those children who want to go on to university through the A-level route, but which remains inadequate and hopelessly complex for those who want to go on through vocational and skills education."

Rishi Sunak, who was Chancellor at the time, argued in his Mais lecture that February: "Providing our people with a world-class education is one of government's greatest responsibilities… education is the most powerful weapon we have in our fight to level up." He is right, but education has fallen down the list of Whitehall priorities. According to the Institute for Fiscal Studies, health spending will have increased by 42 per cent between 2010 and 2025, but education will have risen by less than 3 per cent.

The Times education commissioner Lord Bilimoria, the founder of Cobra beer and president of the Confederation of British Industry, said failing to invest in education was "the biggest false economy," but just pouring more money in was not enough. "There's got to be a shift of mindset," he said. "We need to unleash the creative potential that lies within almost every child in this country. If it is that ability to be creative and innovative that makes us more competitive as a country, then we've got to turbocharge that. We're not even scratching the surface of tapping into it."

The entrepreneur Sir Richard Branson, who is dyslexic, said too many children, particularly the most disadvantaged and those with special educational needs, were being failed by "one size fits all" schools. Putting less emphasis on exams and more on employment skills would be "better for the economy" and "better for the individual," he told the commission. "For countries that have already done it, it is already giving them an economic boost."

The inventor Sir James Dyson told the commission that there was an urgent economic imperative for reform to the curriculum and assessment system to produce the entrepreneurs and engineers of the future. "Children are creative, they love building and making things… but as they get closer to GCSEs and A-levels, all that is squashed out of them," he said. "It's all about rote-learning, not about using your imagination."

The rapid rise of online schooling during the pandemic showed the power of technology to boost learning but also highlighted the fact that British education is still in many ways an analogue system in a digital age. "It's as if it's still selling DVDs in the age of streaming and Netflix," the former Conservative education secretary Justine Greening said.

The World Economic Forum put critical thinking, problem-solving, creativity, resilience, and initiative in its list of "top ten skills of 2025." In the highest-performing countries, including Estonia, Singapore, and Finland, schools actively seek to prepare their pupils for the future by promoting these skills as well as imparting knowledge.

The Organisation for Economic Co-operation and Development has added "creativity" to the list of qualities that will be assessed — alongside reading, maths, and science — in the next Programme for International Student Assessment (PISA) tests of 15-year-olds later this year. The UK is one of only a handful of countries that has refused to take part, preferring a more traditional approach. Without a change of direction in education, however, "global Britain" will soon be left behind.

The skills children need for life are obvious; we just need to teach them. (The Times)

A Quote from Michael Morpurgo

"We have remarkable teachers all over the country who are guiding our children intellectually and emotionally through all the complexities of growing up, encouraging them, inspiring them, enriching them, and devoting their lives to them. We have thousands of remarkable schools. Yet the system has failed and is failing so many. At the heart of my concerns as a teacher, one way or another all my life, has been that we have a system of education geared to the system, not the child, the teacher, the parent, and the school. Life is not a race, not a competition. It is for living, for finding your own voice, your self-worth, your own place in society."

Times Education Commission Final Report

(https://nuk-tnl-editorial-prod-staticassets.s3.amazonaws.com/2022/education-commission/Times%20Education%20Commission%20final%20report.pdf)

Chapter 19

The Education System In The UK

The education system should not be political, but it is at the mercy of each political party's short-term agendas that fluctuate with their ideology. Education is about supporting future generations with the skills to manage the rest of their adult lives. We need to create well-rounded adults who can innovate and help the economy for future generations. They are also humans with social, emotional and mental needs. Happy individuals will work towards a happier society.

Ofsted 2019

In terms of the health and well-being of our pupils and teachers, the UK education system is arguably near breaking point. Recent reports reveal that up to 54% of teachers state their job often or always impacts negatively on their mental and/or physical health (Ofsted, 2019).

Comparing the Education System to the Fashion Industry

If a shop mass-produces only medium-sized outfits, they can only dress part of the population. Accommodating those who are smaller or larger will cost more if they have to tailor outfits for the sizes they have not included.

Blackadder Goes Forth

Someone described the school as similar to the *Blackadder Goes Forth* programme, a British sitcom set during World War I. The head and the leaders of the academies are in their offices designing curriculums and planning lessons that are removed from the reality of the classroom. Teachers and children are in the trenches dealing with the realities of life and learning, with the parents on the side asking for support for their children.

The orders are sent down from on high via constant emails, instructions, and lesson observations, checking how they teach the children. They are intensively monitored to ensure the teachers are implementing the academy's agenda in accordance with the checklist required by the government and Ofsted.

Death by PowerPoint

Children increasingly lose their Art, Music, and Drama to academic lessons as they sit to listen and read from screens. Some academies have a curriculum that is required to be taught in every school, so at any one time, each teacher in that year is teaching the same information. There is no autonomy for the teacher and no individuality for the children. Some schools have stopped 'Golden Time', usually at the end of the week when children can get out games and toys to play and socialise freely.

Individual talent is required at 18 when they finish their education, but it is not acknowledged or encouraged during their time in schools because the academies are too busy dictating what they think they need to learn in primary schools, teaching geography over emotional and social development.

The UK Education System – Have We Got It Wrong?

Too often in the UK education system, we create environments that can lead to feelings of shame, criticism, guilt and threat – factors that contribute to poor mental health and increase vulnerability to psychological disorders.

Pupils in Estonia massively outperform pupils in England. In 2016, global tests revealed that 15-year-old Estonian pupils ranked 3rd for science and 6th for reading (UK pupils ranked 15th and 22nd respectively). In Estonia, however, the focus on early years education is making children 'school-ready' – this includes both socially and emotionally. This is a world away from the UK, where at age 6, we put our children in formal testing situations and print each school's results in a national league table, something Estonia does not do.

Author - Professor Frances Maratos, Professor of Psychology and Affective Science at Derby University (March 2020) https://www.derby.ac.uk/blog/the-uk-education-system-have-we-got-it-wrong

Alternative Ways

Finnish education offers one of the best education systems in the world. Finland has been voted the happiest country to live in, for five years in a row. Happy people accomplish a lot more in life. In 2021, the UK dropped to position 17 and then to 20 in 2023.

While Finnish PISA performance scores have decreased, they are still high compared to other countries. I think we are seeing in the UK that there are sometimes more important things in life than getting the best score. *Source: A Different Perspective on Finland's Educational Success*

The Three C's

The English education system is based on three Cs: competition, coercion and cramming. The Finnish system has three different Cs: collaboration, communication and conceptualisation. Finnish education is not perfect, and it is not the only route to high PISA performance. But the OECD is in no doubt what a 21st-century education requires: "When teachers feel a sense of ownership over their classrooms, when students feel a sense of ownership over their learning, that is when learning for the information age can take place." There is an alternative, if we so choose. *Chris Sinha, Honorary Professor, University of East Anglia*

Why Do We Take Our Children to School and Expect the Teachers to Do It All?

Review the Curriculum

There needs to be more play and extended learning throughout school. Core subjects such as writing, maths and reading are essential, but the child must know they are valued for who they are. They are uniformed very early and made to sit and listen, which can be intimidating for some, along with the ever-increasing size of schools.

Some academies take the planning away from the teacher and create a generic curriculum that every school must comply with. Constant monitoring and assessment of the teachers ensure that only what the academy wants is delivered, ensuring that the 'one-size-fits-all' lesson is taught. Teachers used to have an element of creativity to tailor their lessons to their classes and pupils.

There need to be planned times for children to pursue their interests and facilitate their learning through those interests. A child will learn when they are motivated. As adults, we have more time for people and are kinder humans when acknowledged for who we are. When you control, cram, and compare people, they turn against each other due to the stress applied. If we don't feel safe, we will not learn.

Poor Hand-to-Eye Coordination

A professor of surgery says students have spent so much time in front of screens and too little time using their hands so that they have lost the dexterity for stitching or sewing up patients.

Roger Kneebone, professor of surgical education at Imperial College, London, says young people have so little experience in craft skills that they struggle with anything practical.

The professor, who teaches surgery to medical students, says young people need to have a more rounded education, including creative and artistic subjects, where they learn to use their hands.

Source: BBC News October 2018

Bullying

The bully is usually bullied or feels unsafe. Schools struggle to deal with it, and parents struggle to acknowledge it. My children are not perfect and neither was I. Children act differently in different situations. I have seen children get away with poor behaviour because the teacher does not believe it happened.

Put people or children under pressure, and they turn on each other; you only have to read *Lord of the Flies* by William Golding.

I loved show-and-tell in Reception, where a child could stand in front of the class and discuss their interests. Schools start like this, but there needs to be more time for individuality. Seeing the other children's faces and enthusiasm for each other was lovely.

You can start to see a child's strengths and talents in their infant years. However, a child who once organised his friends to make a 'hideaway' in the playground or sat for hours building with Lego becomes lost and sad when asked to sit and write. All the other skills go unnoticed, and their mental health dips as the child is judged for not being able to write in a book as being a measure of their intelligence and progress.

The education system is designed to funnel children into higher education. Those who don't get there can do an apprenticeship or a 'T' level; but is this system working?

Key Findings from the CBI – Getting Young People 'Work-Ready'

While progress is being made, employers are still raising concerns about a perceived narrowing of the school curriculum – particularly the decline in creative subjects. In addition, businesses value character and wider skills more than ever.

We know that business has a key role to play in getting young people work-ready. Indeed, 72% of employers are currently engaged with schools and colleges but stand ready to do more.

This report calls on the government to:
1. Rethink qualifications, including GCSEs
2. Broaden the EBacc to include a creative subject
3. Work with the education sector and business to develop a framework and shared approach for essential attributes to sit alongside the Gatsby Benchmarks
4. Integrate its Youth Charter and Careers Strategy

Getting young people 'work-ready' marks a crucial first step in setting out a CBI vision for how education should prepare young people for the modern world. *What is the Confederation of British Industry (CBI)?*

The Confederation of British Industry (CBI) is a non-profit organisation that lobbies on national and international issues on behalf of businesses in the United Kingdom. Founded in July 1965 by a Royal Charter, the CBI promotes the sustainable progress of UK businesses and industry.

Parents

We send our children to school and hope for community and cooperation. We sign an agreement that lays out the expectations of the school, child and parents and states our responsibilities. Better communication and trust between schools and parents would increase confidence and support. Sometimes, parents need to take more responsibility for their children and teachers need to believe what the parents say. As we move into a blame culture, league tables, and government agendas, things have gone wrong.

One of the following challenges for the next generation is AI. AI will only be as good as those who use it, or it will go wrong. We need to send our children into the world with the skills they need to survive and succeed. We have a duty of care to do this for our children.

Our education and those who dictate its agenda must be more in touch with the real world. So many children are giving up on their dreams and wasting their potential because they cannot gain an education in this 'one-size-fits-all' system.

Chapter 20

The Future Of The Education System

The Future

Children are usually ahead of their parents when it comes to the latest technology. They have the time to understand it and the future they are moving into. With the invention of the internet and AI, information is now accessible to everyone. We no longer need a teacher to be our primary source of knowledge; we can just type a question into our phones. Academies are planning curriculums that make children sit more and more.

The future of education may need to be more about facilitation and less rote learning. A child can find out what they want to know at the touch of a button. The adults in their lives need to concentrate on safeguarding and helping them navigate their lives to become mentally resilient, physically healthy and emotionally stable.

A More Holistic Way

Advocating for a more holistic approach to education, one that mirrors the health system, would support the whole child. This approach integrates various disciplines, such as psychology, social work, and education, to provide support for children's development. Let's give children and their families a good and positive start. The child will hopefully travel through their childhood understanding who they are, knowing their strengths, and having a base level of emotional and mental resilience. Investing early in a child's development will give them the skills to be a more rounded person, a good team member, and a positive member of society.

In a hospital, care is centred around the patient—the nurses, doctors, and technicians who care for the person. In schools, there are governing officials, teachers, and support staff. Schools have social workers, educational psychologists, and educational advisers, but they are spread thinly across many academies and are funded when resources are available.

In a hospital, the patient would have access to:
- Physiotherapists
- Occupational therapists
- Dieticians
- District liaison nurses
- Psychologists
- Mental health nurses, with connections to another hospital where patients are seen or referred.

In a school, this all stops with the teachers. If there is an undiagnosed autistic child, it's up to the staff in the school to believe the parents or pick up on the issues if they have the knowledge to do so.

Starting correctly will provide parents with confidence. There must be less of a rush to get children on to the educational conveyor belt.

Play and Exercise

Play and physical exercise are disappearing, but these can be used as a way of learning and should be extended for more years to allow children to feel more secure in their ways of learning. A child will be more motivated to learn if they understand how they learn, whether it is visually, auditorily, or kinaesthetically. Allow a child to see where they struggle so they can play to their strengths. Adults can play a crucial role in supporting a child's learning journey. They are often too focused on knowledge, which is primarily helpful in improving a child's ability to pass a test at the end of their time at school. If you stand back and support a child in learning, they will be motivated to do it for themselves.

Executive Functioning

Show me any adult who has fine-tuned all their executive functioning skills, let alone a five- or 15-year-old child. These are the skills behind how we learn and function in life. It's like giving a challenge to someone without the instructions or skills to complete it. Instead of punishing a child for being unable to sit still, accommodate and provide strategies to support them. They will be empowered and motivated, knowing how they are able to complete a task, even if it means getting up and wandering around the classroom to get ideas to finish it. Schools need to be more flexible when technology is available that could make teaching more creative and fun.

Social, Emotional, and Mental Health Support

A child is not going to learn if they are unhappy. An empowered child sees their talents, feels valued in a system and is less likely to be a bully or be bullied. When people feel valued, they are more likely to support each other. This seems unimportant to the adults who design and implement the educational curriculum. Do the academies think about children and what human beings they produce?

Social Care

If schools had social care and a visiting social worker, then safeguarding would be part of normal support. The view of social support would be something to call upon; parents would not feel they have to struggle with their support and have failed as parents. Parenting can be challenging at times. Some children have to deal with adult issues in their home lives, but school may have no idea about this..

Schools and academies need to have more social and community involvement and transparency.

Mental Health

Mental health support should be provided by a counsellor and not just for six weeks. If there were a hub or community place where parents could come for social support for things that happen in life: divorces, separations, redundancies and death. Parents could come and talk because the common goal is to support the family and identify children's issues.

Make mental health support available early and acceptable from a young age.

There are many situations where a child gets in trouble at school for their behaviour. The child's parents are in the process of separating, and the child is sad. The other children in the class know they can wind this child up; his social circumstances easily trigger him. The child is then told off for disrupting the learning. Children are left processing adult problems and sit in class worrying rather than learning.

Educational Psychologist

Having an Educational Psychologist attached to the school helps children who are not progressing or struggling to settle down at work, saving so much wasted learning time. Many schools do this but have to share resources. Children go under the radar and don't get help because teachers don't know how to identify these children. More involvement would help these children, especially those who never disrupted the class's learning time. Time and support would be there for those who get anxious, and they could be taught ways to manage their anxiety as a life skill instead of being picked up when they have an eating disorder or panic attack in secondary school.

Setting up Future Generations to fail

Vulnerable adults, without support don't see the dangers, especially on the internet. Things become darker and influences in their lives become questionable. They are adults, so parents and carers have no claim or control.

Animals prepare their young for adulthood with survival skills, emotional resilience and mental stability. We are supposed to be the superior species with laws and legislation to help us safeguard our children.

I recently completed my Safeguarding update for my Learning Support Assistant role. This update is mandatory for anyone working with children and vulnerable adults, but I feel as though I am reviewing the sad things that happened to my son at the hand of the education system.

We are failing our children due to a lack of accountability, knowledge, insight and neglect.

Action Needs to Be Taken, and the Agenda Challenged

A multi-disciplinary team around every child who needs it, without putting pressure on the teachers, helps the child and society in the long run. We could transform the health of our nation and reduce the pressure on the health system if we took healthy eating and exercise seriously in childhood. A bit more money, effort, and support will pay off. More support at nursery and starting school allows children with problems or learning difficulties not to be left behind or missed, and parents are involved in the process.

We can have a knee-jerk reaction to issues when they have already happened and the government inquiries when a child is found dead. It's too late for the young adult with no qualifications who is disillusioned and turns to drugs or the child with mental health or eating issues who feels their life is out of control.

Other skills are being neglected, which are more important for the health and well-being of a developing child. We all learn more if it's fun, and then we want to do it.

The time and effort spent ensuring all children are safe and mentally and emotionally ready to learn allows children to be self-motivated, seen, and valued. If children feel valued and value others, there would be less discrimination and bullying. Children who are taught how to work as a team will take this into adulthood. We are supposed to support and educate them to become positive, functioning adults.